CITYSPOTS
DUBR

Helena Zukowski

Thomas Cook

Written by Helena Zukowski
Updated by Arijana Goleš

Published by Thomas Cook Publishing
A division of Thomas Cook Tour Operations Limited
Company registration No: 1450464 England
The Thomas Cook Business Park, 9 Coningsby Road
Peterborough PE3 8SB, United Kingdom
Email: books@thomascook.com, Tel: +44 (0)1733 416477
www.thomascookpublishing.com

Produced by The Content Works Ltd
Aston Court, Kingsmead Business Park, Frederick Place
High Wycombe, Bucks HP11 1LA
www.thecontentworks.com

Series design based on an original concept by Studio 183 Limited

ISBN: 978-1-84157-964-1

First edition © 2006 Thomas Cook Publishing
This second edition © 2008 Thomas Cook Publishing
Text © Thomas Cook Publishing
Maps © Thomas Cook Publishing/PCGraphics (UK) Limited
Transport map © Communicarta Limited

Series Editor: Kelly Anne Pipes
Production/DTP: Steven Collins

Printed and bound in Spain by GraphyCems

Cover photography (Historical Centre) © Müller Bodo/4Cornersimages.com

CONTENTS

SYMBOLS KEY

The following symbols are used throughout this book:

ⓐ address ⓣ telephone ⓦ website address ⓔ email
ⓛ opening times ⓝ public transport connections

The following symbols are used on the maps:

𝐢	information office	▦	points of interest
✈	airport	O	city
✚	hospital	O	large town
🛡	police station	o	small town
🚌	bus station	▭	motorway
🚆	railway station	—	main road
✝	cathedral	—	minor road
❶	numbers denote featured	—	railway
	cafés & restaurants		

Hotels and restaurants are graded by approximate price as follows:
£ budget price ££ mid-range price £££ expensive

ⓞ *Dubrovnik with Lokrum Island*

INTRODUCING
Dubrovnik

Introduction

So many words of praise have been heaped on Dubrovnik, which is known as the 'pearl of the Adriatic', that it has always shone like a beacon in the world of tourism. As part of the former Yugoslavia, it was an enormously popular sun-and-sea destination; no one was prepared for the economic problems that resulted from plummeting tourism during the Balkan wars. Over the past decade, however, the word that Croatia is back in business has been spreading like honey on a hot summer's day. Thanks to the welcoming nature of the Croatians, and a programme of studiously authentic rebuilding, the charm of Dubrovnik has reasserted itself and visitors can experience this captivating culture once again.

Part of the city's eternal allure may be the questions and contradictions that cling to it. How, for example, did Dubrovnik manage to hang on to its majestic city walls in the 19th century when every other city in Europe was tearing theirs down? How do the waters that lap Croatia's rugged coastline remain so incredibly clear and full of fish? How can a country that celebrates religious festivals with such fervour also be Europe's top naturist destination? And how has Dubrovnik managed to remain intact after so many centuries of invasion?

Like Prague, Dubrovnik always kept an eye on the future: when invaders flocked in and threatened to wreak havoc in the city, the citizens paid the conquerors to leave them alone. These invaders, who came from cities such as Venice, Istanbul, Budapest and Vienna, sometimes stayed and put down roots, leaving their imprint on the culture. It's no wonder that the citizens developed a great yearning to be part of the Western world. Now, as part of independent Croatia, the citizens of Dubrovnik feel sure that they will blend seamlessly in when the country joins the European Union in the near future.

Before the 1991 war, Croatia had long been home to minority populations, but in the 2001 census more than 90 per cent of the population identified itself as ethnically Croat. Croats warmly welcome visitors, and are committed to putting the horrors of the war and ethnic tensions behind them. The painstakingly restored Dubrovnik is, once again, in the words of George Bernard Shaw, a 'paradise on earth'.

● Walk on the ancient walls of the city

When to go

The ideal times to visit Dubrovnik are usually May, or the late summer and early autumn months. By then the major tourist push is over, yet the sea will still be warm and the days pleasantly balmy. Average temperatures in May are 23°C (73°F); in September the average is 27°C (80°F) and in October 22°C (72°F). For those interested in lots of activity and enjoying the limited range of nightlife, August is the best month to go, but it can be very hot and crowded then. Dubrovnik in winter has an almost poetic charm: just walking around the city at that time of the year can be an enchanting experience, and it's not too cold – the average January temperature is usually around 9°C (48°F).

SEASONS & CLIMATE

On the Adriatic coast, Dubrovnik enjoys a Mediterranean climate, with hot, dry summers and mild spring and autumn weather. Winter is generally a bit cooler, with occasional rain.

The tourist season generally runs from April to October, with spring and summer the best time to enjoy activity holidays, including biking or hiking. The sea is usually warm enough for swimming between mid-May and early October.

ANNUAL EVENTS
January & February
International Dubrovnik Carnival For the best part of two months, the city gets festive, and the carnival in Dubrovnik is how many people think life in general should be – mainly concerned with dressing up. Details of particular events and locations are available from the tourist information office (see page 152).

February
Feast of St Blaise (3 Feb) The city's patron saint (see page 10)
is celebrated with a procession around town.

March & April
The Procession of the Religious Brotherhoods (Good Friday –
10 Apr 2009; 2 Apr 2010) More ceremonial than religious these
days, but a riot of pomp (and more dressing up). ⓐ Korčula

May–September
The Moreška Sword Dance A tradition that's evolved into a major
tourist draw for Korčula (which is why it's staged once at 20.30
every Thursday during these months). ⓐ Cathedral Square, Korčula
🕓 20.30 Thur, May–Sept

July & August
Dubrovnik Summer Festival (mid-July–mid-Aug) This highly acclaimed
international festival hosts everything from ballet to Shakespeare.
Performances take place in the squares and courtyards of the
Old Town (see page 14).

July
Dalmatian Klapa Festival Klapa is a form of traditional, unaccompanied
folk-singing that's enjoying a huge renaissance in Croatia. Come and
see what all the fuss is about. ⓐ Split ⓦ www.klapa-trogir.com

August
Festival of Creative Disorder (mid-Aug) A festival that caters to
distinctly alternative tastes, with various counter-cultural events
and happenings. ⓐ Split

SAINT BLAISE: THE PATRON SAINT OF DUBROVNIK

If you feel that eyes are watching you as you walk around Dubrovnik, it's likely to be those of Sveti Vlaho (St Blaise), whose image seems to be everywhere. He is the symbol of the Dubrovnik Republic and appears on the state flag and coins, on the cannons that were once placed along the city walls and over gateways into the city. Historically, St Blaise was a 4th-century physician and spiritual leader who, according to legend, saved the life of a child who was choking to death on a fish bone. He thus became the patron saint of people with ailments, particularly sore throats.

While a bishop, in AD 316, St Blaise became caught up in a sporadic anti-Christian campaign that was being waged by the Roman emperor Diocletian (even though the Edict of Milan, passed three years earlier, was supposed to allow Christians the freedom to practice their religion officially). No one is quite sure how he was martyred, but one account claims he was flayed to death with iron combs, which is why a comb is often used as his emblem; he is also the patron saint of wool-combers.

Four centuries after his death, a cathedral priest dreamt that St Blaise had appeared to him, telling him that a fleet of Venetian galleons was anchored off the island of Lokrum near Dubrovnik and pretending to take on water barrels; in reality it was preparing to attack. The priest warned the officials, saved the city, and St Blaise was officially made Dubrovnik's patron saint in 972. St Blaise is celebrated annually on 3 February with holy services and a parade of his relics around the town.

⬥ St Blaise: Dubrovnik's patron saint

⬤ *Fireworks sparkle behind the cathedral tower of St Domnius in Split*

Ladja Marathon (second Sat in Aug) A *ladja* is a type of ancient canoe, and every year over 30 teams of 12 people row a race on a 22.5 km (14 mile) route from Metković to Ploče. Around 50,000 fans line the banks of the River Neretva to enjoy the spectacle.

August & September
Quarantine (Karantena) From late August to early September, this international multimedia festival features evening performances of

contemporary theatre, music, film and dance. Details of particular events and locations are available from the tourist information office (see page 152).

September & October
Festival of New Film and Video (late Sept–early Oct) A highly-regarded festival that features independent short films from Croatia and full-length foreign releases. ⓐ Split Ⓦ www.splitfilmfestival.hr

December
New Year's Eve Celebrations Both Dubrovnik and Split see the new year in with a bang, with street concerts, fireworks and widespread partying – not one for the lily-livered.

PUBLIC HOLIDAYS
New Year's Day 1 Jan
Epiphany 6 Jan
Good Friday 10 Apr 2009; 2 Apr 2010
Easter Sunday 12 Apr 2009; 4 Apr 2010
Corpus Christi 22 May
Anti-Fascist Resistance Day 22 June
Croatian National Day 25 June
Victory Day and National Thanksgiving Day 5 Aug
Independence Day 8 Oct
All Saints Day 1 Nov
Christmas Day 25 Dec

Dubrovnik Summer Festival

The Dubrovnik Summer Festival is the big one: Dubrovnik's most important cultural festival of the year, bar none. Attracting an international line-up of artists, it's the biggest and best festival, not only in Dubrovnik, but in all of Croatia. Over the years, it has attracted such celebrated names as Herbert von Karajan, Yehudi Menuhin, Zubin Mehta, Monserrat Caballe, Isaac Stern and the Vienna Boys' Choir. Don't expect to see the likes of Take That, though – the Dubrovnik Summer Festival celebrates ballet, opera and jazz (stars like Duke Ellington and Dizzy Gillespie have played here).

The festival was born in September 1950 during a period when many theatrical and musical events were springing up all over Europe. Kicking off mid-July, the 45-day festival makes use of every available space in town for a long list of concerts and theatrical performances that take place in every courtyard, square and bastion. In 1952, Marko Fotez, one of the original group of enthusiasts who started the festival, brought a production of *Hamlet* to the Lovrijenac Fort, and this soon became the favoured setting for the famous Shakespearean classic. Some of the Renaissance-baroque architecture of the town has, over the years, provided equally appropriate backdrops for many classic works such as Goethe's *Iphigenia*, which was staged by the great Croatian director, Branko Gavella, and Vojnović's *The Trilogy of Dubrovnik*, set in the authentic rooms of the Knežev dvor (Rector's Palace, see page 63). And dance companies such as Alvin Ailey, Merce Cunningham and Martha Graham have set their pieces in historical locations.

Tickets for the headliner events usually sell out well in advance, so anyone planning to attend should check out the festival website (Ⓦ www.dubrovnik-festival.hr) as soon as the programme becomes available, usually in April. For some of the smaller performances, there are usually tickets available at the festival kiosks on Stradun (see page 64) and at the Vrata od Pila (Pile Gate, see page 64). It's also a good idea to book accommodation very early since the town fills up quickly at festival time. For more information, phone ☎ (020) 326 100 or email ✉ info@dubrovnik-festival.hr

⊙ *Numerous concerts take place around the city during the Summer Festival*

History

If Dubrovnik knows one thing well, it is that beauty has its price. Almost from its founding in the 7th century, Dubrovnik (formerly known as Ragusa) has been forced to pay off potential conquerors – and indeed continued to do so right up to the 20th century – in order to preserve its internal autonomy or save the city from destruction. Byzantine emperors, Venetian doges, Normans, Hungarians, Turks – all demanded tribute of one sort or another as a price of going away and leaving Dubrovnik alone.

By the 15th and 16th centuries, Dubrovnik was experiencing a Golden Age with a merchant fleet that ranked third in the world and a ruling class that spent lavishly on the arts. However, when the great earthquake of 1667 either destroyed or damaged every building in the city, Dubrovnik was already experiencing a downturn; by now England and Holland dominated the seas and trade had shifted to the Americas. There was chaos after the quake as people fled in panic rather than trying to control fires. It was said that pupils were heard crying for help from beneath the rubble of their school, and there was looting everywhere. When the city was finally rebuilt, it was in the white stone that dominates today rather than the elaborately wealthy Renaissance style of before. For the next two centuries Dubrovnik was caught between adversaries, as the Hapsburg Empire battled with the Turks and Napoleon with Russia, each empire crashing in its turn.

When the Hapsburg Empire was finally pulled apart in 1918, Dubrovnik was incorporated into the newly created Yugoslavia. This hobbled along through recessions and hardships until World War II, when Communist partisans became the only effective force against the Axis occupation. After Dubrovnik was liberated in 1944, it became part of the Republic of Croatia, a semi-autonomous unit within Yugoslavia under Marshall Tito. Here it remained until the final collapse of Communism in 1989.

In 1991, with the United States refusing to recognise Croatian independence and Serbia pushing for a unified Yugoslavia, war once again broke out. The Yugoslav army began its attack on Dubrovnik on 1 October, overrunning tourist resorts in the south, shelling targets within the city and destroying the airport and the seaport at Gruž. The bombardment lasted until May 1992 when finally, once again, Dubrovnik's beauty saved the day. Since the city had been declared a World Heritage Site and its city walls recognised as Europe's best, there was a huge global outcry at this terrible destruction. The attacking forces retreated, but they left behind a city with almost all of its hotels damaged in one way or another, and much of the rest scarred from mortars or shelling.

Dubrovnik has started again. The city authorities have been whittling away at the immense debt incurred from the war and working with UNESCO to repair damaged buildings and restore Dubrovnik to a state of beauty. In 2007 it was officially reported in Parliament that all key buildings that could be saved had been saved and restored. Dubrovnik is back in business.

⬣ *The city was rebuilt with white stone*

Lifestyle

Croats see themselves as belonging to the Western world, even though in terms of religion the country stands between Islam and Orthodox Christianity in the East and the Catholicism of central Europe. The official language, according to the Constitution, is Croat, but in the large cities and along the coast most people speak at least one foreign language (usually English, though this is sometimes complemented by German and/or Italian).

When meeting a Croatian, it's usual to shake hands, although a kiss on the cheek is appropriate when it's a friend. Croatians tend to be friendly but not obsequious – shopkeepers and waiters are not universally helpful. In conversations, tread carefully when the 1991 war comes up: it can be a conversational minefield, since years of intermarriage have blurred any clear dividing lines between Serb and Croat. The country's cultural heritage is a safe subject that will make you friends.

As a visitor, casual clothing when sightseeing and on the beach is usual, but churches frown on anything scanty – legs and shoulders should be covered (this is not a rule, but will save embarrassment). For business, appearance is important: this means a suit and tie for men and business dress for women. Restaurants and nightclubs don't require this kind of formality, but Croatians always try to look their best when eating out. One place where you don't have to worry about dress is at one of the many nudist beaches (these have signs with the letters FKK on them). At family beaches, it is OK to go topless, except when going into a beachside bar or restaurant, when tops should be worn.

When it comes to food, Croatians usually eat lunch relatively late in the afternoon, so restaurants have a kind of daily brunch called

🔴 *Young Croatians regard themselves as Western Europeans*

marende that's available in the morning. (It's similar to lunch, but with smaller portions.) Pizzerias, perhaps as a legacy from the years of Venetian rule, are everywhere, and no Croatian town is without one. Another legacy, this time from Hapsburg rule, is a love of pastries. Local *slastičarnice* (patisseries) are filled with tortes and rolls and lots of goodies stuffed with whipping cream. At meal times, Croatians usually clink glasses and look directly into each other's eyes while cooing '*Živjeli*' (which translates as 'all the very best').

Culture

Having experienced hundreds of years of foreign occupation, Croatia has a rich and multifaceted cultural heritage that has left Greek and Roman ruins overlaid with later layers of Venetian Gothic and Hapsburg splendour. This influence is seen clearly in the architecture and cathedrals, particularly in the work of such sculptors as Juraj Dalmatinac of Zadar in the 15th century. Dalmatian artists worked closely with Italian artists, adopting the Italian Renaissance style, and much of their work sits today in international museums. Also of Dalmatian origin was the 20th-century sculptor Ivan Meštrović, whose simple, emotionally powerful work won him many admirers, including Rodin. A large collection of his sculptures can be seen at his former home in Zagreb.

Croatian literature, like its art, was strongly influenced by the Italian Renaissance and flowered in the Dalmatian region. One of Dubrovnik's most famous writers, Ivan Gundulić, was born in the late 16th century. He is considered Croatia's greatest poet. His epic poem, *Osman*, which celebrates the Polish victory over the Turks in 1621, is a Croatian classic. The plays of 16th-century playwright Marin Držić (after whom the theatre in Dubrovnik is named, see page 32) are still performed and enjoyed today. Among more contemporary writers, Miroslav Krleža is a giant; a novelist and playwright whose books have been translated into English. Ivo Andrić, born in Bosnia of Croatian parents, won the Nobel Prize for Literature in 1961 for his work, which includes *The Bridge on the Drina* (1945).

Dubrovnik's annual highlight is the Summer Festival (see page 14), when the whole town becomes a stage. International figures in the worlds of opera and music come to perform at the 45-day festival that culminates in a huge fireworks display. The cultural scene for

⬣ *The Marin Držić Theatre*

● *Traditional folk dancing and music in Čilipi*

the rest of 'the season' (roughly May to October) is equally rich: Dubrovnik has its own symphony orchestra, theatre groups and dance ensembles. The indefatigable symphony performs year-round in a number of venues, such as the Revelin Fortress (see page 32), just outside the Ploče Gate, and the Sveti Spas (Church of Our Saviour) on Stradun, just inside the Pile Gate. Throughout the summer there are impromptu open-air rock and jazz performances.

Folk dancing and folk music are tremendously popular with young and old alike. The massive popularity of the **LADO Ensemble** (Ⓦ www.lado.hr), a folk collective who turn up every year at the Summer Festival and routinely bring the house down, shows that traditional culture is of huge importance to Croatians. Dubrovnik is also home to one of the country's most famous folk troupes – the 300-strong Lin o Ensemble.

🅾 *Dubrovnik's main beach is near the old part of the city*

Shopping

As a shopping destination, Croatia is not the trendiest place, but does produce some interesting items that are good to take home as gifts or for your store-cupboard. Croatia has had a long tradition of skilled handicraft production, the best examples of which tend to be lace work and embroidery. The latter is found almost everywhere: a characteristic design is red stitching on a white background, used on table linens, pillowcases and blouses. Pag lace (see page 135) is the most famous in the country, and is made using skills dating back to the Renaissance.

⬤ *The farmers' market in Dubrovnik offers delicious local produce*

TIE ONE ON

Of all the millions of businessmen who knot their ties each morning, few realise that the wearing of a tie actually began in Croatia. It all started in the early 17th century, when Croatian soldiers started wearing narrow scarves tied loosely around the neck. When foreign soldiers came to Paris during the Thirty Years War, among them were Croatian mercenaries who were wearing their scarves. The Croatians' stylish neckties impressed the French, always on the lookout for a fashion statement, so by 1650 neckwear ' la croate' had hit the court of Louis XIV. This phrase evolved into la cravate. Not long after, King Charles II, in exile in France, fell in love with the style. When he returned to England he took it with him as the height of culture and elegance.

Two shopping centres have sprung up near the harbour at Gruž, **Shopping Centar MINČETA** (⬧ Nikole Tesle 2) and **Shopping Centar Srđ** (⬧ Obala Stjepana Radića 25). Neither presents any radical retail revelations, but they can be useful.

Local food and drink products will be high on most shoppers' lists. The local variety of olive oil can be bought all over the city, and when it's mixed with herbs it makes a fabulous present (or medicine!). Lavender and other herbs made into fragrant oils or bound into sachets make a good and inexpensive gift. Some of the best lavender products come from the island of Hvar (see page 126). Another good (if heavy) gift are the stone products from the island of Brač, which are usually in the form of candlesticks, ashtrays or vases. Penkala writing instruments (named after Slavoljub Eduard Penkala, the Croatian inventor of the

USEFUL SHOPPING PHRASES

What time do the shops open/close?
Koliko je zatvaraju otvaraju/trgovine?
`Ko-li-ko ye `zat-va-ra-yoo ot-va-ra-yoo/tr-`go-vine?

How much is this?
Koliko to košta?
`Ko-li-ko to kohr-shta?

Can I try this on?
Mogu li to probati?
Mo-goo li to `pro-ba-ti?

My size is ...
Moj broj je...
Moy broy ye...

I'll take this one, thank you
Hvala, uzet ću ovo
Hva-la oo-zet choo o-vo

**This is too large/too small/too expensive.
Do you have any others?**
Ovo je preveliko/premalo/preskupo. Imate li nešto drugo?
O-vo ye `pre-ve-li-ko/`pre-ma-lo/`pre-skoo-po. `I-ma-te li ne-shto droo-go?

first mechanical pencil and the first solid-ink fountain pen) can be found in most stationery stores and tourist shops, as can ties and cravats – Croatia just happens to be their birth place (see page 25).

Some of the best souvenirs tend to be edible or drinkable, particularly wines and speciality liqueurs such as Bremet liquor or brandies with herbs in the bottles. Croatian wines are not well known abroad, mainly because they are produced in such small quantities, but they are surprisingly good, as is *rakija*, a distilled spirit made from a grape base that is normally drunk as an aperitif or digestive. Among the white wines, good choices are Pošip and Grk (from Korčula, see page 76), Vugava, Malvazija and Traminac. For reds, try the Dingač, Plavac and Babić.

Cheeses are excellent, particularly those from the island of Pag, or goat's cheese from Lika, but be sure to eat them before you return or buy sealed packages to avoid confiscation at Customs. Croatian *tartufi* (truffles) and truffle-based products (like oils) are a good buy, as are herbal teas, which are usually available freshly dried in the markets. Do buy some onions – the sweet, sweet onions of Croatia are a very special treat. *Ajvar* is another taste sensation: a red, creamy paste made of ripe red peppers that is wonderful on sandwiches or with cold cuts. You can buy it in jars. For the sweet tooth, *paprenjak* is a traditional aromatic pastry made of honey, walnuts and pepper that even comes in specially designed boxes or bags.

🔽 *Croatian cloth of varied colours is a typical souvenir*

Eating & drinking

When it's mealtime, look for a *restoran, restauracija* or *konoba* (tavern). A *gostiona* (inn) is a more basic version of a *restoran*. For Croatians, the most important meal of the day is *ručak* (lunch), which they eat relatively late in the afternoon. For visitors, lighter meals (low-cost, smaller portions) are available during the *marende*, a kind of brunch snack.

For a picnic lunch, the nearest open-air market or *samoposluga* (supermarket) will carry the bread, cheese, meats, fruit and vegetables that you need. Bread can be bought at a *pekarnica* (bakery) and sandwiches can often be made up on request. *Lisnato tijesto* is puff pastry filled with cheese, meat or vegetables. *Burek* (a pie filled with meat or cheese) and *čevapčići* (grilled 'kebabs' served in a flat bread bun called *somun*) make a quick, tasty snack.

In Dubrovnik, and all along the Dalmatian coast, plain, grilled seafood dishes are the big favourite; all are seasonal and supremely fresh. The classic is grilled fish served with olive oil and lemon with *blitva sa krumpirom* (swiss chard and potatoes with garlic and olive oil) as an accompaniment. Another favourite is shellfish *na buzaru* (quickly cooked with white wine, garlic and parsley). Shellfish not to miss here are *ostrige* (oysters) and *dagnje* (mussels).

Croatians like to serve their cheese first, before the main meal, often with *pršut*, a home-cured ham from Istria or Dalmatia, and

PRICE CATEGORIES
Price ratings are for a basic meal of main course, salad and a drink.
£ up to 60kn   ££ 60–100kn   £££ over 100kn

◖ *Enjoy the café culture of the city*

olives. This typical and delicious delicacy goes through a long process of cleaning, salting, hanging and smoking; it will melt in your mouth. *Paški sir* comes from the island of Pag (see page 134) and is a hard, piquant cheese that has a taste somewhere between Parmesan and mature cheddar. Soups are usually clear and light and served with very thin noodles.

For main courses, grilled or pan-fried chops are popular, and come either plain or as a *bečki odrezak* (schnitzel), or *Zagrebački odrazak* (stuffed with cheese and ham). *Mješano meso* (mixed grill) is on most menus and consists of pork or veal cutlet, a few rissoles of minced meat and perhaps some spicy *kobasica* (sausage). Lamb is often prepared as a spit-roast; you can sometimes see a whole lamb being cooked beside the restaurant. Stews reflect the central European heritage, with *gulaš* (goulash) done as a sauce over pasta and *pašticada* (beef in vinegar, wine and prunes). Italian-influenced risottos are a popular accompaniment to the main course, especially 'black risotto', made with squid ink.

For dessert, try a Dubrovnik speciality called *rožata*, the local crème caramel. Other typical desserts include *sladoled* (ice cream), *torta* (cake) and *palačinke* (thin pancakes, which are usually filled with marmalade, walnuts with cream or chocolate sauce).

Most restaurants serve wine by the glass, carafe or bottle, while *kavanas* have a full range of alcoholic and non-alcoholic drinks as well as pastries and ice creams. A *kafić* is a smaller version of a *kavana* and usually caters to a younger crowd. Cafés and café-bars open early for that mandatory morning espresso and start serving alcohol from 09.00. The usual closing time is 23.00, although they sometimes stay open later in the summer.

Pubs tend to look a bit British; they serve both local and imported beers. Croatian beers are usually high quality – two good local brands are Ožujsko and Karlovačko, or Tomislav, which is a domestic dark beer. Croatian wines, both red and white, are good, with the best of them being from the Pelješac Peninsula or from Korčula (try the fruity dry whites from Pošip and Grk). *Prošek* is a sweet wine, tawny red in colour, which is usually chilled with an ice cube or two. *Travarica* is a strong grappa flavoured with herbs, *lozovača* is grappa made from grapes, while *šljivovica* (brandy) is made from plums.

Service charges aren't usually included in the bill, so the common practice (as when paying for a taxi, too) is to round up the bill to the nearest 10 kuna or up to 10 per cent on bigger bills. If the service has not been good, then it's up to you whether you tip or not.

USEFUL DINING PHRASES

I would like a table for ... people
Trebam stol za .... osoba
Tre-bam stol za ... `o-so-ba

May I have the bill, please?
Platiti, molim?
`Pla-ti-ti mo-lim?

Waiter!/Waitress!
Konobar!/Konobarica!
Ko-no-bar!/ko-no-ba-ri-tsa!

Could I have it well-cooked/medium/rare, please?
Molim vas za mene dobro pečeno/polupečeno/
na engleski način?
*Mo-lim vas za me-ne do-bro pe-che-no/`po-loo-pe-che-no/
na `en-gle-ski na-chin?*

I am a vegetarian. Does this contain meat?
Ja sam vegetarijanac. Da li ovo ima mesa?
Ya sam ve-ge-ta-ri-ya-nats. Da li ovo ima me-sa?

Where is the toilet (restroom) please?
Molim vas, gdje je WC?
Mo-lim vas gdie ye ve tse?

I would like a cup of/two cups of/another coffee/tea
Molim jednu/dvije/još jednu kavu/jedan/dva/još jedan čaj
*Mo-lim yed-noo/dvie/yosh yed-noo ka-voo/ye-dan/dva/
yosh ye-dan chay*

Entertainment & nightlife

The big entertainment events are staged in the warm summer months, the most notable being the huge Dubrovnik Summer Festival (see page 14). Adding to the rich cultural environment, there are informal open-air pop and jazz concerts in the Old Town during the high season, and special events at the town's two main cultural institutions – the **Marin Držić Theatre** (ⓐ Pred Dvorom 3 ⓘ (020) 428 946), which specialises in serious drama (Croatian), and the Dubrovnik Symphony, which holds concerts year-round at the Knežev dvor (Rector's Palace, see page 63). The grounds of the Revelin Fortress just outside the Ploče Gate are another popular venue (for all show details, phone ⓘ (020) 351 800). Tickets for the symphony can be bought from the DSO office on Starčićeva 29 or via ⓦ www.dso.hr

The **Kino Sloboda** (ⓐ Luža 1 ⓘ (020) 323 372) is the city's main cinema. In Lapad, **Kino Slavica** (ⓐ Ponedjeljak 14) is an open-air cinema, only open during the summer months. Most films are subtitled rather than dubbed into Croatian, and tickets are cheap. However, make sure you look for films made in English-speaking countries, or you may find yourself listening to characters speaking Russian with Croatian subtitles.

The best selection of bars is in the Old Town, with many of them prominent on the popular marbled streets. Wander down some of the labyrinthine alleys to find not only some of the more interesting and less typical bars but also the less crowded and less expensive. The Old Town is lively at night with lots of live music played in the cafés, especially during the summer season, but actual 'nightlife' is a bit thinner on the ground. **Club Lazareti** (ⓐ Frana Supila 8 ⓘ (020) 324 633), out past the Ploče Gate, has the hippest music,

DJs and dancing – they occasionally organise live rock, jazz and ethno gigs as well. There are discos in most major hotels during the summer months, while some city clubs transfer to the open air at coastal resorts during the summer. There's not much information in the local press on events, so the best bet is to ask around or look for posters in town.

● *There are plenty of bars and restaurants in the Old Town*

Sport & relaxation

SPECTATOR SPORTS

Football As in the rest of Croatia, *nogomet* (football) is keenly followed in Dubrovnik. There's a local team called **NK Gošk** (ⓔ Fra F Careva) that was put together by a Dubrovnik entrepreneur. They usually play in the Gradksi Stadion Lapad. The Gradski is on the small side – capacity 7,000 – and in 2007 it was announced that work on a much larger venue was about to begin.

Water polo Water polo is the number-one sport in Dubrovnik, and watching **VK Jug** (ⓦ www.jug.hr), one of the world's best water-polo clubs, is a very popular pastime among Croatians. A league called Divlja Liga plays during the summer, with each team representing one of Dubrovnik's beaches. Half-serious, half-fun, this is for amateurs only and everyone can join in. If you want to play, contact the attendants on your beach.

PARTICIPATION SPORTS

Climbing Croatia has had a long climbing tradition and was among the first seven nations in the world to found a national climbing organisation. For more information on where to pursue this sport, contact the **Croatian Climbing Federation** (ⓔ A Kozarčeva 22, Zagreb ⓘ (014) 823 624).

Extreme sports Lovers of extreme sports might want to try paintball, or even bungee-jumping from the elegant Franjo Tuđman suspension bridge. You don't have to book, just turn up with your courage any time between 1 May and 1 October. It's near the modern port of Dubrovnik, west of the Old Town in the suburb of Gruž. For details call Luci Bilić on ⓘ (020) 418 516

Hiking Hiking is one of the best ways of checking out the beautiful countryside around Dubrovnik. The path above Šipčine will take you up to the top of Mount Sr for an amazing view of the whole archipelago. Other good hikes include several at Župa and on the Pelješac Peninsula.

Horse riding On a sunny day, with the ocean breezes blowing, the place to be is in Konavle (to the south), where they have a number of small horse ranches. **Blue Trail Horseback Riding** (ⓐ Popovice ❶ (020) 798 899, ask for Pero Kojan) organises five-hour treks along the Adriatic coastline.

Water sports With such great lakes and warm coastal water, water sports are big in Croatia – windsurfing, fishing, scuba diving (see page 103), sailing, rowing, water polo, and kayaking. A number of companies, such as **Aurora Maris** (ⓐ A Metohijska 2 ❶ (020) 313 445), have fleets of charter boats for bareboat or skippered sailing. For detailed information, contact the tourist office. For fishermen, there's everything from big-game fishing to fly fishing, but a licence is required. For details call the **Ministry of Agriculture** (ⓐ Marka Majorice 4 ❶ (020) 332 393).

RELAXATION

If you're partial to post-workout euphoria, there are two fitness centres in Dubrovnik:

Fiziofitness Lapad ⓐ Kardinala Stepinca 18 ❶ (020) 436 899 Ⓜ Bus: line 5

Wellness Dalmacija ⓐ Grandvilla Argentina F Supila 14 ❶ (020) 440 596 Ⓜ Bus: line 8

Accommodation

Dubrovnik has been in the hotel business in one form or another since 1347, and has survived through many vicissitudes. During the siege of Dubrovnik, however, the city lost around half of its hotel availability. Thankfully, the accommodation situation is improving fast.

If you want to stay right in the city centre, there is not a massive choice. There are excellent options outside the Old Town, though, and these are at most a short walk or bus ride away from the centre. If money is no object, there are some great places overlooking the sea just east of the town walls; while in the mid-range there are a number of options on the Lapad Peninsula, about 3 km (nearly 2 miles) from the centre, or in the Gruž port area. If you have access to a car, you can look at some of the pension-style places in the villages around Dubrovnik.

During the summer season, there's a big demand for rooms, especially by tour groups who block-book, so independent travellers should book well in advance. Prices in the highest season (July and August) can be 20 per cent or more higher than winter or off-season rates.

A word of warning: anyone arriving via ferry or bus is likely to be swamped with offers of unlicensed rooms, and while some of these

PRICE CATEGORIES

Gradings used in this book are based on cost per person for two people sharing the least expensive double room with en-suite bathroom and breakfast in high season (July & August).

£ up to 200kn   ££ 200–500kn   £££ over 500kn

may turn out to be OK, others may be a long way from the centre of town and have all sorts of hidden 'extra costs' associated – so be careful.

HOTELS

Orhan £ Small, 11-room hotel with basic (but spotless) rooms. Nice location in a quiet cove below a fortress. Good restaurant. ⓐ Od Tabakarije 1, under Old Town ❶ (020) 414 183

● *The charming Hilton Imperial (see page 40)*

Zagreb £ Great value in this small 2-star hotel with clean rooms in a lovely old building. ⓐ Šetalište Kralja Zvonimira 27, Lapad ⓘ (020) 436 333 Ⓝ Bus: line 5 from Pile or 6 from Gruž

The Berkeley ££ A family-owned hotel that opened its doors in June 2007 and offers 20 studio and one-bedroom apartments. Excellent. ⓐ Ulica Andrije Hebranga 116A ⓘ (020) 494 160 Ⓦ www.berkeleyhotel.hr Ⓝ Bus: line 8 from Pile

Dubrovnik ££ A 3-star hotel by the beach in Uvala Lapad, just 7 km (4 miles) from the old town. Has its own tennis courts. ⓐ Šetalište Kralja Zvonimira bb ⓘ (020) 435 030 Ⓦ www.hoteldubrovnik.hr Ⓝ Bus: line 7 from Gruž or 6 from Pile

Hotel Argosy ££ Situated in the heavenly oasis of Babin Kuk, we're talking greenery, we're talking fragrant, we're talking great value. Good for children. ⓐ Iva Dulčića 41 ⓘ (020) 446 100 Ⓦ www.valamar.com Ⓝ Bus: line 7 from Gruž or 5 and 6 from Pile

Lapad ££ Once a graceful summer villa, this large hotel has good basic rooms and public areas that echo its former life. Small swimming pool. ⓐ Lapadska obala 37 ⓘ (020) 432 922 Ⓦ www.importanneresort.com Ⓝ Bus: line 9

Neptun ££ On the Babin Kuk, this ten-storey building has south-facing rooms, most with a sea view. Its bright, self-contained, airy rooms are good for families. Near the beach. ⓐ Kardinala Stepinca 31 ⓘ (020) 440 100 Ⓦ www.hotel-neptun.hr Ⓝ Bus: line 5

Stari Grad ££ This charming little hotel within the city walls has only eight rooms, but it also has a superb upper terrace where you can

eat your breakfast while enjoying panoramic views over the bay.
ⓐ Od Sigurate 4 ⓣ (020) 321 373 ⓦ www.hotelstarigrad.com

Argentina £££ This is another rejuvenated 5-star hotel with
a swimming pool and beach area. It has fine views towards
Dubrovnik Old Town and is within walking distance of the centre.
ⓐ Frana Supila 14 ⓣ (020) 440 555 ⓦ www.hoteli-argentina.hr

Bellevue £££ Located atop a cliff overlooking the Adriatic, this
modern five-storey property is situated just 800 metres (nearly
half a mile) from the city centre. ⓐ Pera Čingrije 7 ⓣ (020) 330 000
ⓦ www.hotel-bellevue.hr ⓝ Bus: line 4 from Pile

Excelsior £££ A 5-star hotel with all the trimmings, fabulous views
and balconies facing the sea. ⓐ Frana Supila 12 ⓣ (020) 353 353
ⓦ www.hotel-excelsior.hr

◔ *The Excelsior's magnificent sea view*

Hilton Imperial £££ Just a few steps away from the Pile Gate, this 5-star hotel, which was created out of two 19th-century palaces, has all the comforts you could wish for (including an indoor swimming pool) and an intriguing history: George Bernard Shaw and H G Wells stayed here. ⓐ Marijana Blažića 2, near Old Town ⓣ (020) 320 320 ⓦ www.hilton.com

Pucić Palace £££ Once an 18th-century palace, this is now a 5-star hotel standing right on the main market square within the city walls. Plush and fully equipped. ⓐ Od Puča 1 ⓣ (020) 324 111 ⓦ www.the pucicpalace.com

Villa Wolff £££ A first-class beach hotel in the Bay of Uvala Lapad, ten minutes by car from the Old City walls, it combines the comfort of a hotel stay with the peace of a private residence. ⓐ Nika i Meda Pucića 1 ⓣ (020) 356 432 ⓦ www.villa-wolff.hr ⓝ Bus: line 4 from Pile

YOUTH HOSTELS
Youth Hostel £ Between Gruž and the Old Town, this hostel has bunk-bed accommodation in four- to six-person dormitories. Basic breakfast on the terrace or kitchen facilities, but call in advance because it books up quickly in the summer. ⓐ Just off Bana Jelačića at V Sagrestana 3 ⓣ (020) 423 241 ⓔ dubrovnik@hfhs.hr ⓝ Bus: line 7 from Gruž or 4 from Pile

PRIVATE ROOMS
There is a huge supply of private rooms in Dubrovnik, and these can offer very good value for money as a budget option if you want to stay right in the centre. Dubrovnik travel agencies can be contacted

by email to book a room, or you can check a number of on-line resources (try Ⓦ www.dubrovnik-apartments.com).

Apartment Anuška ££ Situated on Lapad Peninsula, Anuška is minutes away from fab beaches, clean sea, beautiful walking areas and rich Mediterranean vegetation. ⓐ Batala 1 ⓣ (020) 526 3155 Ⓦ www.dubrovnikapartment-anuska.com Ⓝ Bus: line 6 from Pile

Apartments Within Medieval Walls ££ Not, perhaps, the snappiest of titles for four apartments in a building just inside the city walls; but the rooms are lovely. ⓐ Bandureva 1 ⓣ (020) 323 433 Ⓦ www.karmendu.com

Dubrovnik Apartment ££ Should you be seeking a room in a lovely stone house that's surrounded by a garden filled with flowers and is owned by a charming couple, no further need you look. ⓐ Janjinska 14 ⓣ (091) 507 1320 Ⓦ www.apartmentdinkadubrovnik.com

CAMPSITES

Camping Solitudo The best (if the only) site in the area offers exposure to nature alongside 300 pitches, a pool, a restaurant and tennis courts. ⓐ Vatroslava Lisinskog 17 ⓣ (020) 448 249 Ⓦ www.camping-adriatic.com Ⓝ Bus: line 7 from Gruž or 5 from Pile

THE BEST OF DUBROVNIK

A break in Dubrovnik will soothe your senses. Here you can enjoy the beauty of an ancient walled city, the startlingly clear blue waters of the Adriatic, the taste of superb fresh seafood and the sound of silence.

TOP 10 ATTRACTIONS

- **The city walls** A stroll along this aerial promenade of Europe's best city walls guarantees panoramic views of the Adriatic and glimpses of the rooftops and alleyways of the town (see page 58)

- **Franjevački Samostan (Franciscan Monastery)** Home to Croatia's most beautiful medieval cloister, the friary also has a history as a pharmacy dating back nearly 700 years (see page 60)

- **Korčula** A verdant isle that provides a taste of traditional Croatian life and has an attractive town with a Venetian flavour (see page 76)

- **Cavtat** Accessible via a glorious boat trip and once the ancient city of Epidaurum, this is now a charming, palm-fringed resort (see page 88)

- **Renaissance features** The Old Town in particular is a riot of Renaissance flourishes (see page 58)

- **Mljet** Hop on a ferry and enjoy the peace and quiet of the vast national park (see page 98)

- **Stradun** Head to the main street that's at the heart of action in Dubrovnik, and spend a morning window-shopping, sipping cappuccino, and watching the world stroll by (see page 64)

- **The Old Port** You won't taste fresher fish anywhere than at a restaurant right next to the market (see page 72)

- **The Elaphite Islands** Among the Adriatic coast's beautiful sandy beaches, these have the cleanest and clearest water (see page 92)

- **The oysters of Mali Ston** For lovers of seafood, these little rascals are an unmissable treat (see page 106)

▼ *The Rector's Palace, once the heart of the Ragusa Republic*

Suggested itineraries

HALF-DAY: DUBROVNIK IN A HURRY

With only half a day to spare, the best move is to lace up some walking shoes and start with one of Dubrovnik's key selling points: the walk around the city walls (see page 58). You'll get sea views to the island of Lokrum and a great cityscape of the Old Town. Take a look at the Vrata od Pila (Pile Gate, see page 64), and then have an espresso on the terrace of one of the lovely cafés just outside. Visit the superb Katedrala (Cathedral of the Assumption, see page 60) and, if there's time, head down the Stradun and check out Europe's oldest continuously operating pharmacy in the Franjevački Samostan (Franciscan Monastery, see page 60).

1 DAY: TIME TO SEE A LITTLE MORE

In addition to the sites suggested for the half-day tour, the Dominikanski Samostan (Dominican Monastery, see page 60), with its stunning Renaissance pieces, is highly recommended. A tour of the Stradun is also very enjoyable, with a checklist of the Old Town's best historic sights, such as Velika Onofrijeva Fontana (Onofrio's Great Fountain, see page 64) and the Sinagoga (Synagogue, see page 46). St John's Fortress houses the Pomorski Muzej (Maritime Museum, see page 68), which gives an overview of Dubrovnik's seafaring past. If it's very hot, then why not take a taxi-boat to the island of Lokrum and enjoy an afternoon of swimming and relaxing on the beaches there?

2–3 DAYS: TIME TO SEE MUCH MORE

After spending the first day of your break in the Old Town, take a trip to the Elaphite Islands, a short ferry-ride from Dubrovnik.

The islands were a popular summer retreat for Ragusan nobles, and hiking through the pine woods with the scent of rosemary and sage in the air is a real delight. The three principal islands in the group, Koločep, Lopud and Šipan, each have their own special quality, but all have sleepy villages surrounded by olive groves and grape vines. Koločep has a good sandy beach for swimming in the clear Adriatic Sea. You can stay overnight here and explore all three islands, or spend the third day in Cavtat, a charming fishing village set in a stunning bay around 30-minutes' boat ride from Dubrovnik.

LONGER: ENJOYING DUBROVNIK TO THE FULL

With more time, a day or two on Korčula provides a stunning diversion. A lush island covered in vineyards and ancient buildings, Korčula was the birthplace of Marco Polo in 1254. A 'big city' visit to Split is also recommended, to take in the Roman ruins and history. For seafood-lovers, a stop in Ston to sample mouth-watering, ultra-fresh oysters is also a must. Or you can visit the stunning **Neretva Delta Nature Park** (ⓦ www.neretva.info).

⬤ *Take some time to relax beside the clear waters of the Adriatic*

Something for nothing

In Dubrovnik, the best things in life really are free: the views, the architecture, the sheer beauty of the town itself. Churches, cathedrals and monasteries abound here and admission fees are usually nominal. **Crkva Svetog Vlaha** (❷ Pred Dvorom 3), the baroque church dedicated to the city's patron saint, St Blaise (see page 10), contains a statue of him holding an early model of the city. There's also a lone 15th-century sinagoga (synagogue) on Žudioska Street, the second oldest of its kind in Europe. It contains 17th-century furnishings, Torah scrolls and other artifacts from a once-flourishing Jewish community.

Indoor and outdoor markets are high on the 'free list', and Dubrovnik's two daily ones are always a big draw for photographers. The old market on Gundulićeva poljana has everything from vegetables and flowers to fish and lace, while the main city market caters largely for local people. Another good subject for holiday snaps are the fountains in the city – Velika Onofrijeva Fontana (Onofrio's Great Fountain, see page 64) and Mala Onofrijeva Fontana (Onofrio's Small Fountain, see page 65), plus a number of others.

What about testing your balance for free? Just outside the entrance to the Franjevački Samostan (Franciscan Monastery) cloister (see page 60), there's an unusual stone with a gargoyle face that sticks out from the main wall. The ritual is to stand face to wall on this stone, arms outstretched, for as long as possible without falling off.

If you need a break from history, pick up a picnic lunch and head for one of the beaches (like the pebbled Banje beach) for a day of romping in the Adriatic's crystal-clear waters.

The streets themselves offer no end of surprises: you can step out of a church like St Blaise's and find a troupe of entertainers giving a folkloric show, or turn a corner and discover a group of thespians in Renaissance costume shooting a television series. There are also performance spaces and galleries that feature local talent in the stone buildings and courtyards known as the *Lazareti* (once quarantine houses for travellers during the Renaissance).

🔺 *Magnificent Onofrio's Great Fountain*

When it rains

Even though Dubrovnik chalks up many sunny days, it does rain every once in a while, so it's a good idea to save leisurely inspections of the interiors of the city's many churches for a drizzly day. Crkva Sv Spasa (St Saviour's Church, see page 58) and the Katedrala (Cathedral of the Assumption, see page 60) were both built as 'thank-yous' – the former for deliverance from an earthquake and the latter for deliverance from a storm.

If it's pouring, you can devote plenty of time to discovering the Franjevački Samostan (Franciscan Monastery, see page 60), with its Romanesque cloister and arches topped with carved human heads and fantastic animals. And the pharmacy at the entrance of the monastery is actually one of Europe's most famous. Still functioning, it dates back to 1317 and calls itself the oldest pharmacy in Europe.

Damp days are also a good time to hit the galleries in Dubrovnik, and one very good one is **War Photo Limited** (➌ Antuninska 6 ➊ (020) 322 166), which is run by a former war photographer, Wade Goddard. The gallery specialises in first-rate temporary exhibitions that feature the work of the world's greatest war photographers. It's not for the very young or the faint-hearted: War Photo Limited sees itself as an educator in the field of war photography, with a mission statement that aims to look at war 'as it is': raw, frightening and venal. There are several other galleries worth visiting during cloudbursts, including the Museum of Modern Art (see page 65), which features paintings and sculptures by some of Croatia's best artists.

The Palaca Sponza (Sponza Palace, see page 63) is also an enjoyable rainy-day destination. Built in the 16th century, it was originally used as the custom house and mint, and stages interesting exhibitions.

Shopping for some Croatian delicacies is also a terrific way to while away any periods of rain.

◆ *The fine cloisters of the Franciscan Monastery*

On arrival

TIME DIFFERENCE

Croatia follows Central European Time (CET). During Daylight Saving Time (late Mar–late Oct), the clocks are put ahead one hour.

ARRIVING

By air

Most international flights end in Zagreb with a connection on to Dubrovnik. There are two or three flights a day between the cities and they take one hour. Dubrovnik Airport is around 20 km (12 miles) east of the city, close to the village of Čilipi. A Croatia Airlines airport bus makes regular runs between the airport and the city centre that take about 25 minutes, and there are also taxis readily available – see ⓦ www.taxiservicedubrovnik.com for details. Buses back to the airport leave the bus station 90 minutes before each Croatia Airlines departure. There is no tourist office in the airport, but there is a bank, post office, car-rental office and duty-free shop.
Dubrovnik Airport ⓣ (020) 773377 ⓦ www.airport-dubrovnik.hr

By rail

Perhaps rather surprisingly, Dubrovnik does not have a train station. The furthest towards the city that you can get by train is Split. From here, there are buses to Dubrovnik. See ⓦ www.croatiabus.hr for details.

By road

The bus station is in the port suburb of Gruž, 3 km (nearly 2 miles) west of Old Town. Long-distance buses come straight to the bus station; there is one direct bus a day from Frankfurt, Trieste and

IF YOU GET LOST, TRY...

Excuse me, do you speak English?
Oprostite, govorite li engleski?
O-`pro-sti-te `go-vo-ri-te li `en-gle-ski?

**Can you tell me the way to the bus station/taxi rank/
city centre (downtown)/beach?**
Možete li mi reći kako mogu doći do/autobusnog kolodvora/
taksi-stajalişte/centra grada/plaže?
*`Mo-zhe-te li mi re-chi ka-ko mo-goo do-chi do`
`a-oo-to-boos-nog `ko-lo-dvo-ra/tak-si `sta-ya-li-shta/
tsen-tra gra-da/pla-zhe?*

Can you point to it on my map?
Možete li mi to pokazati na planu grada?
`Mo-zhe-te li mi to po-`ka-za-ti na pla-noo gra-da?

Sarajevo. The bus station has Dubrovnik's only left-luggage facility
(☎ (060) 305 070 🕓 04.30–21.00).
Dubrovnik Bus Terminal 📍 Put Republike, Gruž ☎ (020) 357 020

By water
The ferry terminal is just to the north of the bus station (see above).
Year-round, overnight ferries (catamarans during the summer)
depart for Bari, Italy. These depart from Bari at 22.00 and arrive
in Dubrovnik at 06.00; they leave Dubrovnik at 23.00 and arrive
in Bari at 08.00.

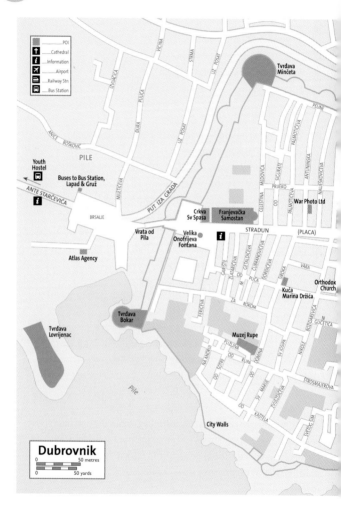

POI
Cathedral
Information
Airport
Railway Stn
Bus Station

VICINA
STRMA
IZ POSAT
Tvrđava
Minčeta

PELINE

RVULACCA
PULCA
PALMOTIĆEVA

ANICE BOŠKOVIC
ĐURA
IZ POSAT
ANTUNINSKA
NALJEŠKOVIĆEVA

PILE

MEDOVIĆA
SIGURATE
PRIJEKO
OD

Youth
Hostel

Buses to Bus Station,
Lapad & Gruž

CELESTINA
War Photo Ltd

ANTE STARČEVIĆA

MILETIĆEVA
PUT IZA GRADA

BRSALJE
Crkva
Sv Spasa
Franjevačka
Samostan
STRADUN
(PLACA)

Vrata od
Pila
Velika
Onofrijeva
Fontana

Atlas Agency

CARFTE
ZLATARICKA
CETALUĆCVA
DUBRANOVIĆEVA
DOBRIĆEVA
VARA
BUDROANOVIĆ
M
PUCA
BOŽIDAREVIĆA

KA
Orthodox
Church

Kuća
Marina Držića
N
GUČETIĆA

ZA
ROKOM

FERICEVA

Tvrđava
Bokar

Tvrđava
Lovrijenac

Muzej Rupe

PUŽLJIVA
OD
SOTE
OD
RUPA
CIMINA
SV JOSIPA
NIKOLE
STROSMAJEROVA

NA ANDRU

SV MARIJE
KNEZVIĆEVA

Pile
OD
SV
SVETOG SIM

KAŠTELA

City Walls

Dubrovnik

0 ————— 50 metres
0 ————— 50 yards

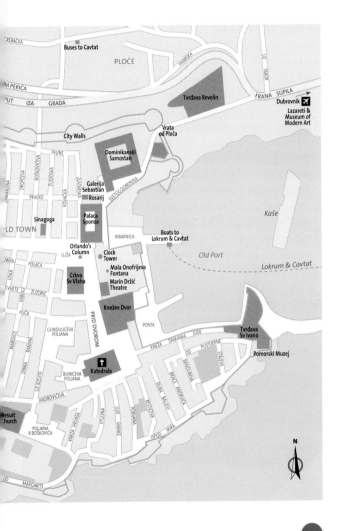

FINDING YOUR FEET

Dubrovnik is compact and easy to navigate once you get a map and see the 'fish skeleton' layout of the streets. Walking around at night is pretty safe, and there's little overt crime. One obvious precaution is to lock up any valuable jewellery, rather than flaunting it on the streets.

The official language of the country is Croatian, but the majority of younger Croats speak fairly good English. Most people working in tourism will have a decent vocabulary, but it doesn't hurt to learn a few words. Croatians appreciate a visitor who makes the effort to communicate in the local language.

Women should note that Croatian men are quite open with their remarks. Most of these can simply be ignored, but if the man persists speak firmly and make your intentions to call for help clear. Drinking in public areas is fine, but there are bars patronised mainly by men, and these should be avoided: a woman alone gives off the wrong signals in this society.

● *Ferries link the islands to the mainland*

ORIENTATION

Tucked into its walls, Dubrovnik's Old Town is tiny, closed to traffic and easy to navigate. To enter the city, there's a choice of three gates: the Ponta Gate at the harbour entrance; the Vrata od Pila (Pile Gate, see page 64) to the west, by the bus station, and the Ploče Gate to the east. Each leads to the Stradun, the marbled 'main drag' that is only 300 m (330 yards) in length and divides the Old Town. Narrow streets and alleys lead off the Stradun, and the street is buttressed by two major parallel streets: Prijeko in the north and Od Puča in the south.

Greater Dubrovnik spreads along the Dalmatian coast from the suburb of Ploče in the southeast to the suspension bridge in the northwest, and across the Lapad and Babin Kuk peninsulas to the west. The main harbour, Gruž, sits between the mainland and Babin Kuk. For maps and details, the tourist office at Dr Ante Starčevića 7 is open Monday to Saturday from 08.00 to 20.00 in the summer months.

GETTING AROUND

On landing at Dubrovnik Airport (see page 50), there are two ways to get into town, 20 km (12   miles) away. For passengers on Croatia Airlines (CA), there's a bus that meets the flight. For departing passengers, buses leave Dubrovnik Bus Terminal (see page 51) 90 minutes before the Croatia Airlines departures. For those who are not flying CA, taxis cost around 220kn if they are metered and around 200kn if you agree a price upfront. For passengers arriving by sea from the port of Gruž, buses (numbers 1A, 1B and 3) run from the port to Pile Gate roughly every half-hour. The number 8 bus runs from Ploče hotels to the Ploče Gate. Local buses cover all of Dubrovnik and run from 05.00 until 12.00 midnight. Tickets are sold at newspaper kiosks or on the bus.

Dubrovnik has a good taxi service as well, with stands at the Pile Gate, Gruž, the bus station and Lapad. You can also get someone to call a taxi to pick up at any of the main hotels. As always, you should check to make sure the meter is turned on before you leave, unless you've pre-negotiated the fare to a particular destination.

To go to any of the islands, take one of the local ferries or a taxi-boat – these travel between Dubrovnik's old port and Lokrum every half-hour in the summer. It's a ten-minute crossing. There are also regular boats to and from Cavtat. All other ferries leave from the main quay on Gruž harbour and are usually operated by Jadrolinija, the national ferry company (see page 126).

CAR HIRE

Hiring a car in Dubrovnik is expensive, at around 500kn a day for an economy car with unlimited mileage. Since the Old Town is so compact for sightseeing, it might not be advisable to rent unless you plan to do some extensive touring around – ferries and buses are a good alternative. The major hire companies have offices in Dubrovnik, but usually you get the best-value rates by booking at home before you leave, either through your airline or on the web. You can try these car-hire companies in the UK:

Autoeurope ❶ 0800 358 1229 Ⓦ www.auto-europe.co.uk
Budget ❶ 0870 1539 170 Ⓦ www.budget.co.uk
easyCar ❶ 0986 333 3333 Ⓦ www.easycar.com
Europcar ❶ 0870 607 500 Ⓦ www.europcar.co.uk
Hertz ❶ 0870 844 8844 Ⓦ www.hertz.co.uk

❶ *Aerial view of the Old Town and port*

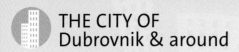

THE CITY OF
Dubrovnik & around

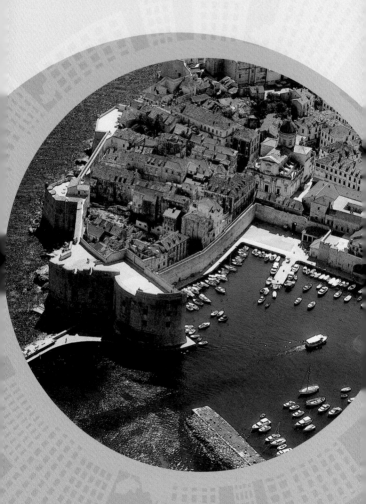

Old Town

Dubrovnik's Old Town is compact and the main sights are close to one another, so that you can see them all without any lengthy stops within a couple of hours. If you have a special interest, say in Renaissance art or musical notation, and want to do a thorough exploration, you should allow at least a half a day.

SIGHTS & ATTRACTIONS

City walls

Depending on whom you talk to, Dubrovnik's city walls (in purple on the map opposite) are the most beautiful, best-preserved, or most complete city walls in the world. It's certainly the place to start any visit to the city. Wrapping themselves around Dubrovnik for just a little under 2 km (1 1/2 miles), they measure 25 m (82 ft) at their highest point and 12 m (39 ft) at the widest.

The whole circuit can be done in a leisurely hour. Begun in the 8th century, building and repairing went on throughout the centuries, including the extensive work that was carried out on them after the 1991 war. There are three entrances onto the walls: one is next to Vrata od Pila (Pile Gate), another on Svetog Dominika leading to the Dominikanski Samostan (Dominican Monastery) and the third on Kneza Damjana Jude near the Akvarij (Aquarium). ⏱ 09.00–19.00 in the summer, with shorter hours in the winter

Crkva Sv Spasa (St Saviour's Church) (see map page 52)

Near Onofrio's Great Fountain, this church was erected as the city's 'thank-you' message after it survived the 1520 earthquake.

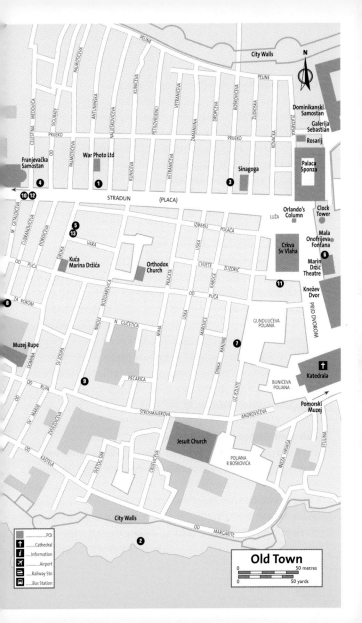

Old Town

0 — 50 metres
0 — 50 yards

| POI |
| Cathedral |
| Information |
| Airport |
| Railway Stn |
| Bus Station |

City Walls

N

PELINE

City Walls

PELINE

Dominikanski Samostan

Galerija Sebastian

Rosarij

Palača Sponza

Franjevačka Samostan

War Photo Ltd

Sinagoga

STRADUN (PLACA)

LUŽA

Orlando's Column

Clock Tower

Mala Onofrijeva Fontana

IZMEĐU POLAČA

Crkva Sv Vlaha

Marin Držić Theatre

Kuća Marina Držića

Orthodox Church

Knežev Dvor

PRID DVOROM

Muzej Rupe

GUNDULIĆEVA POLJANA

Kr Katedrala

BUNIĆEVA POLJANA

Pomorski Muzej

STROSMAJEROVA

ANDROVIĆEVA

Jesuit Church

POLJANA R BOŠKOVIĆA

City Walls

OD MARGARITE

Dominikanski Samostan (Dominican Monastery)

This old structure, dating back to the early 14th century, has two attractions of major interest: its 15th-century Gothic Renaissance cloister, filled with palm and orange trees, and its museum stuffed with a wealth of Renaissance treasures. Of historical interest, there's a painting of St Blaise holding a model of 16th-century, pre-quake Dubrovnik; a splendid Virgin and Child altarpiece, and a Titian altarpiece of Mary Magdalene and St Blaise. ❷ Off Svetog Dominika 4 ❶ (020) 321 423 ❷ 09.00–17.00. Admission charge

Franjevački Samostan (Franciscan Monastery)

Beyond the peaceful and beautiful courtyard, the two most interesting parts of the monastery are the cloister and treasury. The capitals in the cloister are decorated with birds, animals and human faces, one of which is rumoured to be the sculptor suffering from a toothache. The frescoes in the cloister tell the life of St Francis. The friary is also notable for being the oldest continuously functioning pharmacy in Europe: it was founded in 1317. The treasury has relics from the ancient apothecary's shop as well as manuscripts tracing the history of musical notation. Check out the 'balancing stone' beside the west portal. ❷ Stradun 2 ❶ (020) 321 410 ❷ 09.00–18.00

Katedrala (Cathedral of the Assumption)

Located right in the heart of the city, the original cathedral was financed, according to legend, by Richard the Lionheart, after he survived a terrible storm just off the coast near Lokrum. At the height of the storm, the king vowed that – if he survived – he would build a church. Enterprising Ragusan nobles, on hearing of the pledge, sent a delegation to Richard, persuading the king that his money would best be used to build a church in Dubrovnik rather than Lokrum.

◯ *Stradun is the main pedestrian artery of the city*

ⓐ Kneza Damjana Jude 1 ⓣ (020) 323 459 ⓛ 08.00–20.00 Mon–Sat, 11.00–17.30 Sun

Knežev dvor (Rector's Palace)

Twice blown up by gunpowder stored next door, this version of the palace dates to the 15th century and once housed all the major offices of state plus a dungeon (and the gunpowder storage). At the entrance, you walk through pillars made of Korčula marble, one of which is said to be of Aesculapius, the god of healing, who was born in what is now Cavtat. The main door of the palace leads to an atrium in which summer musical recitals are held. ⓐ Pred Dvorom 1 ⓣ (020) 321 437 ⓛ 09.00–18.00

Orlando's Column

This doesn't look all that impressive, but when it was built in 1418 it was the focal point of the city-state, since government ordinances were promulgated here and punishments carried out. A flag with the 'Libertas' motto flies from the top and the start of the Dubrovnik Summer Festival (see page 14) is announced here. The medieval cult of Orlando (Roland) started in the 12th century and was based on the epic poem *Song of Roland*. ⓐ Luža Square

Palaca Sponza (Sponza Palace)

Used as a customs house and mint, the Sponza Palace was built in the 16th century and grew rapidly as Dubrovnik's wealth multiplied. It is elaborately carved with Renaissance arches and Venetian Gothic windows, and currently houses the state archives. Exhibitions are often held inside the majestic courtyard and, during the summer

◀ *The city walls are a great vantage point*

festival, there are concerts. A room dedicated to the defenders who lost their lives during the 1991 war (the Memorial Room of the Defenders of Dubrovnik) is recommended for history buffs. ⓐ Luža Square ⏰ 08.00–13.00

Stradun (also know as Placa)

This is the city's main street, a pedestrian zone that runs from the Pile to the Ploče gates along the line of a channel that once separated the Roman settlement of Ragusa from the Slavic settlement of Dubrovnik. Originally paved in the 15th century (and redone after the earthquake in the 17th), the limestone pavement is polished with centuries of use, so is shiny and extremely slippery when wet.

Velika Onofrijeva Fontana (Onofrio's Great Fountain) (see map page 52)

Just inside the Pile Gate, this fountain, built in 1444, is shaped like a polygon and was once part of the city's water-supply system. Topped by a bulbous dome, there are 14 masks around the fountain that spout water. Visitors to the city were required to wash here to guard against bringing in the plague. There were once statues around the fountain as well, destroyed unfortunately in the earthquake of 1667. Now the main human forms around it are teenagers, who like to gather here to chat. ⓐ Near Pile Gate

Vrata od Pila (Pile Gate) (see map page 52)

This entrance to the Old Town dates back to 1471 and was approached across a wooden drawbridge that was pulled up every night. Today it spans a dry moat with a garden. Just inside the gate is the first glimpse you get of St Blaise, the city's patron saint; nearby stands another statue, of famous Croatian sculptor Ivan Meštrović.

WALKING TOURS

Dubrovnik is an ideal city for walking around, and an hour or two on the city walls is the best way to start. Within the old city, there's a good walk, starting outside the Pile Gate and ending at the Museum of Modern Art. The Pile Gate, which dates back to 1471, has a wooden drawbridge that used to be pulled up every night. Check out the statue to St Blaise and, further on, one by Ivan Meštrović. From here, head to the Stradun, once a marshy channel that separated the Roman settlement of Ragusa on one side from the Slavic Dubrovnik on the other.

Just inside the Pile Gate, spend a bit of time photographing Onofrio's Great Fountain, built in 1444 as part of the city's plumbing system. The Franjevački Samostan (Franciscan Monastery) is next: take a good look at the exterior, but save the interior for a rainy day. At the far end of the Stradun, Orlando's Column in Luža Square symbolises the city's desire for freedom and marked the centre of town when it was built in 1418. On the left-hand side of the square, the Palaca Sponza (Sponza Palace) holds the Memorial Room of the Defenders of Dubrovnik, the state archives and the original workings of the city clock. The clock tower with its astronomical clock is just behind Orlando's Column. Onofrio's Small Fountain, built in 1441, is next to the clock tower. From here, go along the winding Svetog Dominika to the Dominikanski Samostan (Dominican Monastery), out through the Ploče Gate to Lazareti, and take a look at the first-class **Museum of Modern Art** (ⓐ Frana Supila 23 ⓣ (020) 426 590).

CULTURE

Galerija Sebastian

Gallery Sebastian is located in the tiny Church of Saint Sebastian, which dates from 1464. In 30 years' existence, the gallery has organised more than 300 exhibitions by local and foreign artists. ⓐ Sv. Dominika 2 ⓕ (020) 321 490 ⓛ 09.00–20.00 Mon–Fri, 09.00–13.00 Sat, closed Sun

Kuća Marina Držića (Marin Držić House)

This is a theatrical museum, a scientific documentary institute and an exhibition space all rolled into one. It is named in memory of Marin Držić, one of Croatia's greatest playwrights. What makes this museum so unusual is that it's more of a theatrical experience than a museum: visitors find themselves surrounded by puppets, posters and typical stage props. Actors guide people through the exhibits in such a way that they feel like participants of a theatrical performance. ⓐ Široka ulica 7 ⓕ (020) 323 242 ⓛ 10.00–18.00 Mon–Sat, closed Sun

Muzej Rupe (Rupe Ethnographic Museum)

This is a glimpse back to the 16th century: an immense stone barn with 15 huge storage pits that were used for keeping the municipal grain. At one time, these pits were dug into floors all over town, but this is the only one that has survived. The top floor houses an ethnographic exhibition of rural life and husbandry plus costumes, textiles and so on. ⓐ Ulica od Rupa 2 ⓕ (020) 323 013 ⓛ 09.00–19.00 Mon–Sat, closed Sun (summer); 09.00–14.00 Mon–Sat, closed Sun (winter)

◀ *Rupe Ethnographic Museum*

Pomorski Muzej (Maritime Museum) (see map page 52)
Located in St John's Fortress, the Maritime Museum is of great
interest to old salts and those interested in the background of
this seafaring country. It looks at the history of Ragusan sea power,
with model displays of boats throughout the centuries and marine
artefacts. There are trade-route maps, sextants, and a particularly
interesting, well-stocked 19th-century medicine chest, used by
doctors on ships. 🕐 09.00–18.00 in the summer, with shorter
hours in the winter

RETAIL THERAPY

The main artery for shopping is Stradun in the Old Town, where
you'll find clothing and shoe shops in the alleys that run off the
street. There's also a shop where the owner makes and sells candles.
If you are after items that 'say Dubrovnik', the embroidery distinctive
to the Konavle region south of the city is special. You can find napkins
and tablecloths at some of the better gift-shops, but they are pricey.
For traditional Croatian jewellery such as filigree earrings and coral
necklaces, try some of the jewellery shops at the western end of
Puča. Foreigners can claim a sales tax refund within one year for
anything they buy. Be sure to ask the salesperson to fill out the
tax-refund form when purchasing your goods.

There are two fruit and vegetable markets, one in the Old Town
on Gundulićeva poljana and the other one in Gruž. Both sell fresh
produce and are open every day until noon – or sometimes longer.

Alogoritam Books This is the best bookshop in town if you've
finished that novel you brought and need a new book in English.
They also have travel guides and maps. ⓐ Stradun 8 ⓣ (020) 322 044

◭ *Retail therapy is a must in Dubrovnik*

Aquarius Here's the store to get those souvenirs of Croatian music CDs as well as international music. Poljana Paskala 4

Arca Antique Shop For collectors or gift-seekers, Arca has a large selection of antique dishes, vases, glasses, tablecloths and paintings by Croatian artists. Gundulićeva poljana

Art Studio 1 Hajdarhodžić Sells hand-made clay ships and fishing boats; also some paintings and antiques. Zlatarska 1

Euroshop A department store on Gruška obala, close to the market in Gruž. Bus line: 3, 6 or 8 from Pile to Gruž

Franciscan Monastery Pharmacy For a really unusual gift (and to treat yourself, too), stop in at the still-functioning pharmacy to check out the range of unusual lotions and creams, some formulated from recipes dating back to 1317. Some of the recommended are the lemon hand-lotion, rose or lavender face-cream, and the jojoba and menthol moisturiser. If you say it's a gift, they'll give you a special bag. In the monastery near the Pile Gate

Franja Coffee & Teahouse Besides coffee and tea you can pick up great food gifts here, too. There's wild-rose brandy, herbal *rakijas* wine made with the local grapes, figs in honey, olive oil and special liqueurs. Od Puča 9

Ronchi Hats This hat shop has been around since 1858 and has a rich array of, er, hats. Lučarića 2, on a narrow lane near Market Square and Orlando monument

TAKING A BREAK

Buffet Škola £ ❶ A family-run sandwich bar that makes delicious *pršut*-and-cheese sandwiches on home-made bread with locally grown tomatoes. ❷ Antuninska ulica, a side street between Stradun and Prijeko

⬤ *There are many comfy cafés dotted about the Old Town*

Buza £ ❷ Perched on the rocks just outside the Old Town's sea-facing walls, this waterfront bar has atmosphere. Look for the 'cold drinks' sign: serves coffee, *travarica*, cool beer, lemonade and ice cream. ❸ On Iza Mira

Don Corleone £ ❸ There are lots of pizza places in town, but for the best slice to take away this will do nicely. ❸ Boškovićeva 4

Festival £ ❹ Although damaged by war in the 1990s, this is now a smart café with the best sticky cakes and Spanish hot chocolate in town. Excellent café breakfast as well. ❸ Just off the Stradun on Celestina Medovića

Fish Sandwich Bar £ ❺ A venue that has fish and mussel sandwiches for a low-price lunch. ❸ On Široka ulika, next to Proto Restaurant (see page 74) ⏱ 10.00–14.00, 18.00–21.00

Gradska Kavana £ ❻ A cavernous café where locals come for cakes and ice cream on the summer terrace or to listen to live piano in the summer. Lovely atmosphere. ❸ Pred Dvorom 1 ☎ (020) 321 202 ⏱ Café 08.00–02.00 summer, 08.00–00.00 winter; restaurant 10.00–04.00

AFTER DARK

You'll be spoilt for choice in terms of restaurants, with the busiest ones being in Old Town along a street called Prijeko and off Široka ulica. Some of these are closed in the winter. Menus tend to be similar, with heavy emphasis on seafood, grilled meat, pizza and other Croatian specialities like *rižot* (seafood risotto), *meneštra* (minestrone soup) and *buzara* (langoustines in a tomato sauce). Many of the more popular restaurants require a reservation and make a small cover charge.

RESTAURANTS

Kamenica £ ❼ A no-frills eatery and a favourite of the locals for its simple seafood dishes and fresh oysters. ❸ Gundulićeva poljana 8, near the open-air market ◐ All year but closes at 20.00 in the winter

Mea Culpa £ ❽ A popular restaurant, with good pizza cooked in a wood-fired oven and other Italian dishes at cheap prices. Cosy inside, there are also tables on the street and they have draft Guinness on tap. ❸ Za Rokom 3 ❶ (020) 323 430 ◐ 08.00–01.00 summer

Spaghetteria Toni £ ❾ For strong Turkish coffee and what the locals claim is the best pasta (especially the lasagna) in town. Good soups and bruschettas, too. ❸ Božidarevića 14 ❶ (020) 323 134

Gverović-Orsan ££ ❿ Along the Adriatic Road, on the sea in Zaton Mali, 7 km (4 miles) west of Dubrovnik, sits this restaurant. It is housed in a genuine, ancient *orsan* (boat house). ❸ Stikovica 43 ❶ (020) 891 267 ❾ www.gverovic-orsan.hr ❿ Bus: 12 or 15 from Gruž

Marco Polo ££ ⓫ Tiny restaurant, but in the summer you can dine in the courtyard on typical dishes such as *crni rižot* (black risotto in cuttlefish ink). A popular hangout for musicians and actors. ❸ Lučarica 6, on a side street behind the Crkva Sv Vlaha (Church of St Blaise) ❶ (020) 323 719

Atlas Club Nautika £££ ⓬ Located in a building that once used to be the Dubrovnik Nautical Academy, this is considered to be the best place in town for quality seafood. There are grand dining rooms, a small outdoor terrace, formal waiters, crisply folded napkins and an international wine list. **ⓐ** Brsalje 3 **ⓣ** (020) 442 526 or 442 573 **ⓛ** 12.00—00.00 summer, closed winter

Proto £££ ⓭ Right in the centre of Old Town, Proto has been around since 1886 and is known for its fish specialities prepared from old recipes of Dubrovnik fishermen. Formal dining room with relaxed outdoor terrace and meticulous service. Excellent local wine list. **ⓐ** Široka ulica 1 **ⓣ** (020) 323 234 **ⓛ** 11.00—23.00

BARS, CLUBS & DISCOS

Bebap This is one of the few bars in Old Town to stay open after midnight in the low season as well as high. Occasional live concerts. **ⓐ** Knez Damjana Jude, the narrow street leading to the Aquarium

Capitano Swings on Friday nights, especially in the summer with a young crowd. **ⓐ** Pile, just a few steps north of Pile Gate

Divinae Follie On the Lapad Peninsula, this is an open-air disco and the largest club in Dubrovnik. The DJ booth is encircled by the dance floor, which is in turn surrounded by bars. **ⓐ** Put Vataroslava Lisinskog 56, about a 15-minute drive from Old Town **ⓣ** (020) 435 677

Irish Pub Don't expect wearin' of the green or leprechauns: the Irish ale is as far as it goes. It does have a friendly atmosphere and prices are reasonable, so it's popular with students and tourists. You will probably be able to catch midweek football here. **ⓐ** Između polača 5 **ⓣ** (020) 323 992

Latino Club Fuego Probably the most popular club in Dubrovnik, with good music and reasonable prices. ⓐ Brsalje 11, near Pile Gate ⏱ Until 04.00

Libertina Tiny place and a good spot to meet local people. ⓐ Side street next to Sponza Palace

Old Hospital This is just that: an abandoned hospital that has become a club for the younger crowd. Live bands and DJs and a hardcore beat. ⓐ Dr. Ante Starčevića 41

Otok A hangout in Old Town that straddles the chill-out club-cum-speakeasy/art gallery divide with such aplomb that underground artists and mainstream clubbers co-mingle without catfights. ⓐ Pobiljana 8

Sesame Bar A combined hotel and restaurant that has live music on weekends. Fresh oysters from Ston are a speciality. Very intimate interior, but lots of outdoor seating on the upstairs terrace. ⓐ Dante Alighieria, five minutes west of Pile Gate

Talir If you happen to be in Dubrovnik during the Summer Festival (see page 14), this is the place to meet actors and musicians who hang out here before or after performances. Check the walls: photos of Croatian celebrities adorn them. ⓐ Antuninska

Trubadour Hard Jazz Café Intimate pub that flows out onto the surrounding square in high season. This is owned by a former member of a locally famous 1960s beat group called the Dubrovacki Trubaduri – there is live jazz most nights in the summer. ⓐ Bunićeva poljana

Korčula

This is the sixth-largest Adriatic island – and one of the greenest – with a good smattering of vineyards and olive groves. Because of the mild climate, there's a variety of vegetation from conifer forests and meadows of wildflowers to a typically Mediterranean coastline with coves and beaches. The walled town of Korčula, with all its historic associations, is why people mainly come to the island, but it's also interesting as a slice of traditional life. The population here is quite devout and the people observe many ancient religious ceremonies as well as keeping alive folk dances, songs, music and traditional costumes.

Korčula was first settled by the Greeks, but it wasn't until it was ruled by Venice that it became prosperous because of its flourishing shipbuilding industry. Stone was also quarried on the island by skilled local artisans and cut for export. Korčula's growth and expansion was brought to an end after a catastrophic outbreak of the plague in 1529, and the decline continued as Mediterranean trade diminished following the discovery of America. It wasn't until the early 20th century and the development of tourism that Korčula began to emerge from obscurity.

The main Rijeka-Dubrovnik ferry stops at the harbour of Korčula Town, along with other daily ferries making the run from Split to Vela Luka. By bus, there's a daily service from Dubrovnik that crosses the narrow stretch of water between the mainland and the island on a car ferry from Orebić. The bus station is 200 m (219 yards) southeast of the Old Town. The tourist information office (☎ (020) 715 701 🌐 www.czk-korcula.com) is on the western side of the peninsula.

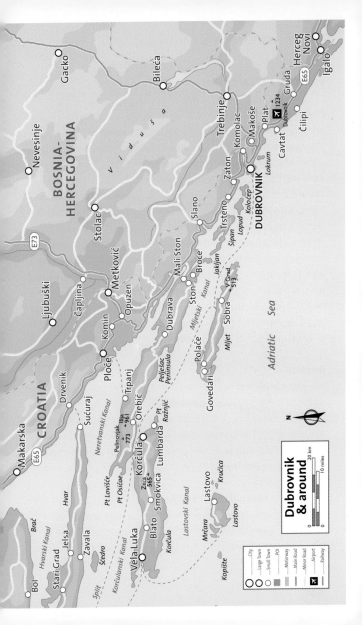

SIGHTS & ATTRACTIONS

From a bird's point-of-view, Korčula Town, the island's main settlement, looks like a fish on a platter with a central spine and ribs branching off on each side. This layout dates back to the 13th century, and was meant to reduce the effects of wind and sun. The town rises above its 13th-century walls like a mini-Dubrovnik. There is a distinct Venetian flavour to the architecture and culture – little wonder, because the Venetians took control of the island in the 10th century and stayed on for more than eight centuries. Most of the buildings date to the town's Golden Age (13th–15th centuries), including one remaining town wall in the south; most of the others were demolished in the 19th century. The town has a special beauty, with its elegant 19th-century staircase sweeping up to Kopnena Vrata (Land Gate), the main entrance to the Old Town. This gate was completed in the 15th century along with the Revelin, the hulk of a defensive tower looming above it.

Beaches

While there are beaches in town, they're usually crowded and rocky, so the best bet is to take the bus to Lumbarda, about 8 km (5 miles) south of Korčula Town – the beaches are a 20-minute walk from the bus station but the great sand on Prižna Bay is worth it. Bilin Žal, just a short distance away, is rockier but has great views of the coastal mountains.

Katedrala Sv Marka (St Mark's Cathedral)

This magnificent 15th-century limestone structure dominates Cathedral Square; it was built in the Gothic-Renaissance style by local and Italian workmen. It has an interesting portal decorated

with a two-tailed mermaid, an elephant and other sculptures. On the façade, there's a beautiful fluted rose window and a strange cornice filled with even stranger beasts. Inside, look for the modern *Pičta* by famous sculptor Ivan Meštrović, and an altarpiece painting by Tintoretto. There's also a bronze statue of St Blaise by Meštrović.

Kuća Marco Polo (Marco Polo's House)

This is a 17th-century house that allegedly marks the spot where Marco Polo, adventurer, merchant and author of the world's first travel book, was born (see below). You can climb up to the tower-like upper storeys for a great view of the terracotta rooftops of the town.

MARCO POLO LIVED HERE, PERHAPS

Despite a shortage of hard evidence, Korčulans insist that their island was the birthplace of the famous explorer. One firm bit of documentation says that Marco Polo was captured by the Genoese in a sea battle off Korčula in 1298; perhaps he was visiting relatives (there is a family on the island named de Polo). Korčulans insist, in any event, that Polo was born in 1254, went to Venice with his family in 1269, travelled the world and then, after being captured by the Genoese, was tossed into jail. It was during this period in jail that he wrote his famous book of adventures. What is certain is that he led an action-packed life, spending 17 years in China as a close personal friend of Kublai Khan. His famous travelogue sparked much interest in the Far East. Wherever he was born, the Korčulans are his biggest fans, and make a point of throwing celebrations to mark the key events in his life.

◢ The magnificent portal of St Mark's Cathedral

(a) Kuća Marco Polo, in the alley Depolo (clock) 10.00–13.00, 17.00–19.00 June–Aug, closed Sept–May

Town walls and towers

The whole town is surrounded by robust 13th- to 15th-century walls and towers: there were a total of 12 in the Middle Ages. There are two principal entrances: Kopnena Vrata (Land Gate) and the Sea Gate on the west. The Revelin Tower, built by the Venetians in the 15th century, is topped with a terrace from which there are excellent views.

CULTURE

Galerija Ikona (Museum of Icons)

A permanent display of icons held by the All Saints' Brotherhood, including a haunting 15th-century triptych of the Passion and Byzantine icons painted on wood, as well as some 17th- and 18th-century ritual objects. (a) Trg Svih Svetih (clock) 10.00–12.00, 17.00–19.00 July & Aug, closed Sept–June

Gradski Muzej (Town Museum)

Housed in a Venetian palace located on the main square, the town museum stands just opposite the cathedral. The collection here includes historical items related to Korčula's history, including a copy of a 4th-century BC Greek tablet from Lumbarda, plus a room upstairs done up to show a typical Korčulan peasant kitchen. (a) Pjaceta (clock) 09.00–13.00, 17.00–19.00 July & Aug; 09.00– 13.00 Mon–Sat, closed Sun, Sept–June

(back arrow) *Green hills and blue seas frame the picturesque town of Korčula*

RETAIL THERAPY

The main things to take home from Korčula and the Pelješac Peninsula are wine and foodstuffs, particularly the produce of the local vineyards and olive groves. wines. Dingač is the area's most famous red wine and is hard to find outside Croatia. Its slightly sweet flavour is reckoned to emanate from the grapes being partially dried before being crushed. It certainly benefits greatly from the area's sun-drenched limestone soils. The best plan is to go directly to the producer at wineries on the island. Olive oils are produced all through the country, but buying directly from the Korčulan grower seems to add a special quality to the oil.

TAKING A BREAK

Cukarin £ ❶ A sweet shop famous for its selection of home-baked biscuits and other delicious goodies. ⓐ In the narrow alley running south from Plokata ❶ (020) 71 10 55

Fresh £ ❷ This restaurant is true to its name and produces fruit-filled smoothies, wraps and their touted Viva!Mex — ground beef, beans and home-made salsa. ⓐ 1 Kod Kina Liburne (between the bus station and the Old Town) ❶ (091) 799 2086

Kiwi £ ❸ A good bet for a cool, soothing ice cream.
ⓐ Just off Plokata 19 Travnja

Grubinjac ££ ❹ An old rustic farmhouse on the way from Korčula to Žrnovo village, with great views over the hills beyond. Meals and snacks can be served on the terrace with the restaurant's home-produced wine. ❶ (020) 711 410

AFTER DARK

RESTAURANTS

Konoba Marinero ££ ❺ Offers home-made specialities and delicious grilled fish in a room filled with maritime bric-à-brac, or out on the terrace squeezed into a narrow alley. ❷ Ulica Marka Andrijića 13 (just off Pjace main square) ❶ (020) 711 170

Morski Konjić 1 ££ ❻ A cosy little restaurant at the northern tip of town; it is hung with fishing nets and serves a selection of meats and fish. ❷ Šetalište Petra Kanavelića ❶ (020) 711 642

Planjak ££ ❼ An established and unpretentious place with a full range of grilled food, especially grilled kebabs. The restaurant has a shaded terrace. ❷ Plokata 19 Travnja, in the centre of Old Town, just a few steps from the main ferry terminal ❶ (020) 711 015

Kanavelić ££–£££ ❽ Specialises in very fresh fish and seafood including mussels washed down with the best local wines. (Try the octopus salad.) Considered formal dining – the grilled scampi are a speciality. ❷ Sveta Barbara 12, near Hotel Korčula ❶ (020) 711 800

BARS & CLUBS

Nightlife in Korčula is limited to a couple of bars and the island's hotels, where live performers entertain guests.

Dos Locos A bar with lots of outdoor seating and a lively atmosphere. ❷ Šetalište Franje Kršinića

Olea A favourite with young people, visitors and locals both. A friendly, sometimes boisterous atmosphere. ⓐ Located between the bus station and Old Town on Prolaz tri Sulara

ACCOMMODATION

HOTELS & GUESTHOUSES
Badija £ Located on the island of Badija and reached by taxi-boat from the harbour, this is a restored monastery. Think 'austere' – but there's a beach and sports facilities. ⓐ Badija Island ⓣ (020) 711 115

Bon Repos ££ On the road to Lambarda, this is a large hotel complex with pool and comfortable rooms. ⓣ (020) 726 880

Korčula ££ This is the oldest of the town's hotels and was the town hall during Austrian times. The rooms are comfy, if slightly frayed. ⓐ Šetalište Franje Kršinića ⓣ (020) 711 078

Park ££ This hotel won't win any architectural awards, but there is a beach and many of the rooms have balconies. ⓐ Šetalište Franje Kršinića ⓣ (020) 726 004

APARTMENTS
With hotel accommodation distinctly limited in Korčula Town, there are at least a number of private rooms and apartments available. It's best to deal with one of the agencies in town that do the booking for these, such as **Marko Polo** (ⓐ Biline 5 ⓣ (020) 715 400 ⓔ markopolotours@markopolotours.hr) or **Turistička Agencija Korčula** (ⓐ Just off Plokata 19 Travnja ⓣ (020) 711 067 ⓔ marketing@htp-korcula.hr).

⬥ *The narrow streets of Korčula Town*

Cavtat

Sitting on a peninsula between two bays, Cavtat (pronounced 'tsavtat') lies about 16 km (10 miles) south of Dubrovnik and makes a good day trip or short visit. Even though Cavtat is popular with packaged tours, the hotel area is away from the village centre so the place still exudes a bit of charm. The seafront promenade is lined with bars, restaurants and palm trees, giving it a decidedly Mediterranean feel and about 1 km (half a mile) east of the town centre there's a *žal* or beach area.

Originally a colony founded by Greeks and known as Epidaurum, Cavtat went through the usual period of invasion and pillaging before establishing itself as a fishing village. It was rediscovered during the days of the Austro-Hungarian Empire at the beginning of the 20th century and became the playground of the rich.

Bus number 10 runs to Cavtat from Dubrovnik every hour, and there are a couple of ferry companies, with varying timetables, that serve the route. For people visiting Croatia by car, Cavtat is a good alternative to staying in Dubrovnik: the accommodation tends to be more reasonably priced and there are no parking problems.

SIGHTS & ATTRACTIONS

The town's best beaches lie to the east and west, about 1 km (half a mile) to the east where all the large package hotels are, and to the west in front of the Hotel Croatia (see page 91). There are also pleasant walks around the headlands where you can swim off the rocks.

Funerary sights may not be on everyone's 'must-do' list but there is one that should be seen. Sitting on a beautiful hilltop overlooking the sea, the showpiece is the Račić Mausoleum, built by famous sculptor Ivan Meštrović for the daughter of a wealthy ship-owning family (it was rumoured that Meštrović was her lover). This white marble sepulchre was built in 1922 and is an eclectic mix of angels, eagles, dogs and so on. After the monument was completed, the entire family died in quick succession.

AFTER DARK

RESTAURANTS
Konoba Kolona £ A budget restaurant serving tasty fare. Shady terrace near the bus stop. ⓐ Put Od Tihe 2 ⓣ (020) 478 787

THE TALENTED MR BUKOVAC
Formerly the home of Vlaho Bukovac, a talented painter born in Cavtat, **Galerija Bukovac** (ⓐ Ulica Vlahe Bukovca 5 ⓣ (020) 236 950) is now a gallery dedicated to his works. Bukovac studied in Paris and travelled widely through Europe before returning to Croatia and playing an important role in the development of Croatian art. His paintings – portraits as well as many other subjects – combine a photographic realism with touches of impressionism. Bukovac ended his career as a professor of fine arts in Prague.

In the centre of town, the 16th-century **Rector's Palace** (ⓣ (020) 478 556) holds more of Vlaho Bukovac's work, along with drawings by Croatian and foreign artists, old coins, and a lapidarium with Roman stone pieces from the 1st century AD. It is also known as the Baltazar Bogisic Collection, after a lawyer and cultural activist who spent his life promoting Croatian literature and learning.

△ *Deliciously fresh fish is served everywhere in the region*

Feral Restaurant ££ Good food and entertainment each weekend.
ⓐ Ante Radica 66 ❶ (020) 478 034

Konavoski Dvori ££–£££ For a grand meal out, this is a highly praised restaurant beside a working watermill on the River Ljuta about 18 km (11 miles) east of Cavtat. Waitresses are in the local Konavali costume and specialities of the house include lamb and trout. ⓐ Pridvorje Ljuta, Konavle ❶ (020) 791 039

Leut ££–£££ Right in the centre of town, this restaurant has been around for three decades serving fresh and delicious seafood. An outdoor terrace is open in the summer months. ⓐ Trumbićev put 11 ❶ (020) 478 477

ACCOMMODATION

Albatros ££ This is one of the beachfront hotels that caters for package holiday guests. It has a private swimming pool and rooms have air-conditioning. ❶ (020) 479 833

Hotel Supetar ££ Right in the centre of town, on the harbour front, this is an older hotel that has been tastefully modernised. ⓐ Dr Ante Starčevića ❶ (020) 479 833 ⓦ www.hoteli-croatia.hr

Hotel Croatia £££ This is a huge, 482-room, 5-star hotel on the ridge of the Sustjepan Peninsula. It offers all the amenities: TV, air-conditioning, swimming pool and private beaches, nudist and otherwise. ❶ (020) 475 555 ⓦ www.hoteli-croatia.hr

The Elaphite Islands

This string of 'car-less' islands, 14 in all (three of which are inhabited), lies between Dubrovnik and the Pelješac Peninsula. They are considered one of Croatia's 'best-kept secrets'. What they offer is an area of rich vegetation, unspoiled nature (their name means 'deer') and a long architectural heritage. Dotted here and there are 15th- and 16th-century Gothic and Renaissance churches together with some pre-Romanesque chapels. Dubrovnik, with its shifting cultures, casts a strong influence over the Elaphites and their villages.

Ferries leave several times a day from Dubrovnik for the main Elaphite islands. Once there, visitors get around on foot, since cars are not allowed. For Lokrum there are boats leaving on the half-hour every day during high season and on weekends from the port in Dubrovnik's Old Town. Out of season, there are people with private boats who may take you across. Ask around.

SIGHTS & ATTRACTIONS

Koločep

Less than a half-hour away by ferry, this is the first of the inhabited Elaphite Isles and a very easy day trip. There are two small villages, Donje Čelo and Gornje Čelo, on an island that is just over 2 1/2 sq km (1 sq mile) in area and that has a population of around 150 people.

The biggest attractions here are the walks through sweet-smelling pine and deciduous forests, with perhaps a picnic halfway through. In season (after May) there are a couple of restaurants on the waterfront where you can end the day eating freshly grilled seafood. The only accommodation on the island is the **Villa Koločep** (❶ (020) 757 025), a group of eight modern units above Donje Čelo beach.

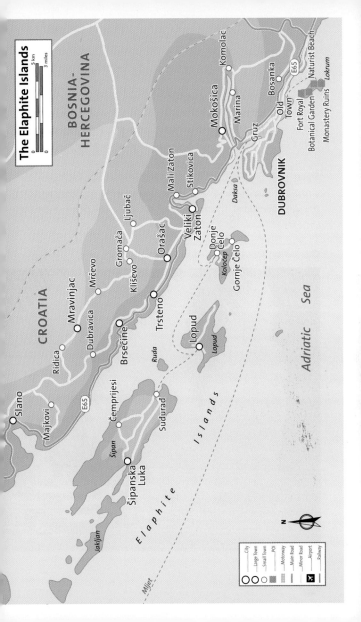

Lopud

Just beyond Koločep, Lopud was once a lively retreat for the noble families of Dubrovnik and remnants of their palatial houses can still be found. On the northern end of the island, the village of Lopud curves around a wide bay and a sandy beach.

Šipan

Šipan, aka 'The Golden Island', is the largest of the Elaphites, and yet the least developed. The main attraction here is the peace, quiet and

🔽 *Lopud was once a favoured retreat for noble families*

gentle walks, especially the 7 km (just over 4 mile) walk from Suđurađ to Šipanska Luka on the island's northern end, which passes groves of figs, grapes and olives. There's a small sandy beach here and some good isolated spots for sunbathing, as well as a fine ruined villa on the harbour front.

CULTURE

The main relic of Lopud's more vigorous past life is a fortified Franciscan monastery and Crkva Gospe od Špilice (Church of Our Lady of the Rocks) with its collection of altar paintings. The small

LOKRUM – PARADISE, CROATIAN STYLE

Lokrum is a tiny island, just 2 km (1 1/4 miles) long. According to local legend, one of its earliest famous visitors came a trifle unwillingly. Richard the Lionheart, on his way home from the Crusades in 1192, encountered a fierce storm offshore. Like others facing shipwreck, he vowed that – if he was saved – he would build a church in thanks. He landed on Lokrum to fulfil his promise, but was persuaded that his money would be better spent if he built in Ragusa (Dubrovnik) rather than on an insignificant island.

Just 15 minutes by boat from the quay in Dubrovnik's Old Town, subtropical, uninhabited Lokrum is wonderfully undeveloped. Peace and tranquillity reign, and the biggest attractions are the beaches (cleaner and less crowded than Dubrovnik) and a network of trails that crisscrosses the island. Lokrum also has a protected naturist beach, one of the country's premier nudist beaches, on the southeastern end, and a warm, saltwater lake. The island has a great variety of flora including an old Botanical Garden with palms, cacti, vines, Australian eucalyptus, ancient trees and herbs running rampant. The garden was established in 1959 as an experiment to see if tropical plants would grow from seed and thrive in a Mediterranean climate.

Fort Royal is a fortress in the Lokrum hills, built in the shape of a star by the French in 1806. It's a steep, 20-minute hike up rickety steps, but from the top there are great views of Dubrovnik, Cavtat and the islands.

museum and treasury at the end of the harbour has a series of 9th- to 11th-century frescoes in bad condition, some icons and other sacred objects and an assortment of other historic bits and pieces, from 500-year-old pudding bowls to 200-year-old French bayonets. Steps lead up to a ruined palace and private chapel built for Miho Pracat, a somewhat legendary 16th-century ship-owner and merchant who allegedly saved Spain from starvation and made himself a fortune at the same time. His bust stands in the Knežev dvor (Rector's Palace) in Dubrovnik (see page 63).

In Šipan, ruined villas are scattered all over the island, remnants of an era when Dubrovnik was powerful, along with ruined churches going back many centuries. In Suđurađ, the ferry's first stop, there are the ruins of a summer palace built by a 16th-century ship-owner.

ACCOMMODATION

There are no hotels or restaurants on Lokrum. In Lopud, the tourist office (🕑 May to mid-Oct) has a list of rooms for anyone wishing to stay longer than a day, and there are two hotels, the **Lafodia** (🛈 (020) 759 022) and **Villa Vilina** (🛈 (020) 759 333). Private rooms are available on Šipan Island for overnighters and there is a harbour-side hotel, the **Šipan** (🛈 (020) 758 000). There are a couple of bars and a restaurant in the hotel and absolutely no nightlife on the island.

Mljet

Mljet, perhaps Dalmatia's most beautiful island, with its steep rocky cliffs, has remained almost untouched through the centuries and has a mystery or two. Even though Malta lays claim to the legend of Calypso and Ulysses and the visit of St Paul after a shipwreck, Mljet may be a more likely base for the stories. Once called Melita, it was infested with snakes until the 19th century and St Paul was supposedly bitten by one (Malta has no snakes). The mongoose was imported to Mljet to control the snake. The mongooses flourished and multiplied, thereby curing the snake problem but causing a mongoose problem in the process. The island's vast National Park (see page 100), which occupies the entire western end of the island, is what mainly draws visitors to Mljet. It can be done in a day trip. A single road runs the length of the island.

The crossing from Dubrovnik takes four hours on the daily Jadrolinija ferry and in the summer one-and-a-half hours on the fast catamaran that leaves Dubrovnik in the morning and returns in the afternoon. The ferries dock just to the east of Sobra and there are buses that take you into town, but there can be a problem in the summer when there are more passengers than buses. For day-trippers, the catamaran will dock at Polače. To get away from transportation headaches, the best idea is to book an all-inclusive package deal from one of the travel agencies; these include ferry, a tour, a chance to swim and a trip out to the island on the lake.

Aside from the buses that meet the ferries, there's no local transport. However, you can hire bikes, cars or scooters from several outlets, the biggest of which is the Hotel Odisej (see page 102) in Pomena. For more information on Mljet contact the tourist office in Polače (❶ (020) 744 125).

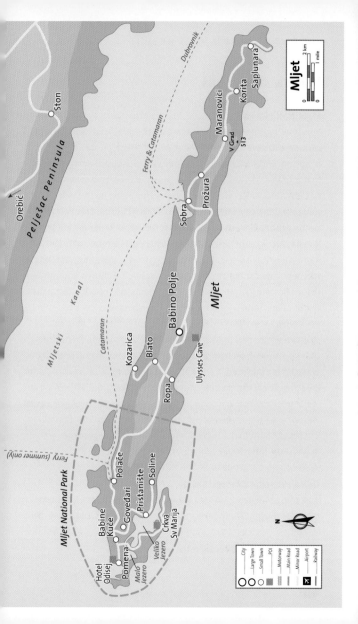

SIGHTS & ATTRACTIONS

Mljet National Park

This is a Croatian national treasure and beside the peace, the lack of commercial development is the main attraction on the island. Since it was never ruled by Venice, no trees were chopped down to build major towns, so the pine and oak forest with its two saltwater lakes has remained unspoiled. The larger of these two lakes, Veliko Jezero (Big Lake), has an island with a charming – but run-down – 12th-century monastery that still displays bits of its Romanesque and Renaissance architecture. The monastery was a hotel in its last incarnation but, since being returned to the Benedictines, restoration has begun and there are Sunday services in the church. You can visit the monastery gardens when they are open and there is a restaurant on the island where lunch is served. The island also has a ten-minute walk where you can gather wild asparagus in the summer or visit two simple chapels built by sailors. There are boats in Pristanište that shuttle visitors back and forth to the island several times a day, with the fee included in the national park entry. A network of paths crisscross the park for walking or mountain biking, and there's a 9 km (5 1/2 mile) trail that runs around the perimeter of the lakes. For a great view of the Pelješac Peninsula and the island of Korčula, there's a steep path up to the highest point in the park, Montokuc.
Ⓦ www.np-mljet.hr

Odisejeva spilja (Ulysses' Cave)

According to legend, Ulysses stayed here for seven years during his epic voyage. Whether this is true or not, there is a cave directly

🔾 *The island of Mljet is beautiful and unspoilt*

south of Babino Polje that can be explored by boat (the easiest way) or by trekking across the fields for a half-hour or so and climbing down to the cave.

Polače

The main attraction of this harbour town are the remains of a Roman palace with fortifications that lie just above the town, and the ruins of an ancient Christian basilica in a sheltered bay.

Saplunara

This stunning sand beach below a small village of the same name is a great day trip or two- or three-day getaway, if you can find accommodation. Families let rooms during the season and there are a couple of basic fish restaurants – and for total relaxation, you can get rid of clothes at a long, deserted, sandy nudist beach that is a 20-minute walk from Saplunara.

TAKING A BREAK

In Pomena, a favourite docking site for yachtsmen, there is a string of small restaurants along the harbour and in Polače there are a couple of small restaurants, a provisions store that is open in the mornings and a bakery. The restaurant at the monastery also serves good lunches.

ACCOMMODATION

Hotel Odisej ££ in Pomena is a modern 3-star hotel that is open from Easter until November. It has 150 rooms, some with a balcony and sea view. The hotel lies in the national park and is a 15-minute

A DIVER'S PARADISE

Jacques Cousteau praised the Adriatic Coast as one of the world's greatest dive locations and for good reason: the coastal waters are crystal clear and hold some very good dive attractions. One of these is an ancient Roman vessel where little remains but some amphorae; a more modern location is a German U-boat. Divers must pay an initial fee of 100kn at one of the registered dive centres or at the local harbourmaster's office before they can dive. For novices, there is an increasing number of dive shops opening up all along the Adriatic coast, offering lessons, equipment rental and guided trips. Around Mljet, diving is restricted to organised groups. For more information on diving, contact the **Croatian Diving Federation** (ⓐ Dalmatinska 12, 10000 Zagreb ⓦ www.diving.hr).

walk from Malo Jezero, so it's a good base for a hiking holiday. ⓐ National Park ⓣ (020) 744 022 ⓦ www.hotelodisej.hr

Private rooms and campsites that are clean and comfortable are available in Pomena and Polače at reasonable prices, but these should be booked in advance. The tourist office in Polače (ⓣ (020) 745 125) can supply the names of people who will rent rooms. For booking ahead, try **Mini Brum** tourist agency (ⓣ (020) 285 566) in Babino Polje. There are also campsites in Babino Polje and in Ropa and a few run by private individuals. Ask a local for more information.

Pelješac Peninsula

This is one of those places that people can often pass straight through without knowing what they're missing. Geographically (see map on page 99), it's a long, narrow peninsula – 62 km (39 miles) long but never more than 7 km (4 1/2 miles) wide. It feels like an island, though, and there's the sense of always being near water. Isolated and undeveloped, Pelješac is mainly known for its two excellent wines (Postup and Dingač), both of which can be tasted in cellars that are open to the public in the summer. Ragusa (Dubrovnik) owned the peninsula from the 12th to the early 19th century, and many of the Republic's finest seafarers came from this region.

Buses from Dubrovnik bound for Korčula make stops at Ston and Orebić three times a day, but to really explore the peninsula properly, a rental car is recommended.

SIGHTS & ATTRACTIONS

Orebić

With its history as a trade centre for 500 years, Orebić has a colourful seafaring past and was once quite prosperous, earning money from building ships to supply a merchant fleet. Today it's a centre for tourism mainly because of its beaches, excellent climate and its proximity to a number of hiking trails. There are some attractions, like the 15th-century Franjevački Samostan (Franciscan Monastery) that is located about a 20-minute walk out of town, with its famous (and allegedly miraculous) icon, *Gospa od Angela* (*Our Lady of the Angels*). It was believed the icon would protect mariners from shipwreck, and there are numerous votive offerings from sailors and sea captains who believe it was the Lady who saved their lives.

◆ *Excellent wines are produced on the peninsula*

There is also a Virgin and Child by Nikola Firentinac, the 15th-century Renaissance master, who also designed the dome at Šibenik Cathedral.

There's a great view of the Pelješac channel from the monastery terrace.

STON – DEFINITELY WORTH ITS SALT

This fortified town has a split personality: Mali Ston is on the north coast and Veliki Ston on the south coast. The most impressive feature in Veliki Ston (sometimes called simply Ston) are 14th-century walls that were built to defend Dubrovnik's northern borders. These stretch across a rugged hillside. Ston doesn't look like much at first glance because rebuilding has been slow since the 1996 earthquake, but this small village attracts visitors and people from Dubrovnik en route to Korčula. They come to eat the fresh, succulent oysters produced in Mali Ston Bay that are prepared in a dozen and one ways, from raw and slippery to baked in delicate sauces. While oysters take top billing, restaurants feature ultra-fresh fish dinners as well.

Historically, Ston's major importance was as a salt-producer: when Napoleon invaded Dubrovnik he was as keen to get control of Ston's salt as he was to occupy Dubrovnik. Twenty of the original 40 towers along the fortifying walls – and 5 km (3 miles) of the walls themselves – are still standing, and from the top you can get great views of Mljet. There are some interesting Gothic and Renaissance houses here too.

About a 15-minute walk away is Mali Ston. It doesn't have a beach, but you can swim in the clear water from the jetty or rocks. To the north there's a ruined fortress with steps leading to a parapet and great views.

AFTER DARK

RESTAURANTS

Restaurant Mlinica ££ Nice place for a nibble, on the ground floor of the Ostrea hotel (see page 108). ☎ (020) 754 555 ⓦ www.ostrea.hr

Kapetanova Kuća ££–£££ On the waterfront of Mali Ston, this was once the residence of a captain of the guards. Good seafood menu and a wide selection of wines. ☎ (020) 754 555 ⓦ www.ostrea.hr

Vila Koruna ££–£££ Both a hotel and a splendid restaurant right on the water. It serves oysters and seafood freshly chosen from stone tanks that sit under the plate-glass windows on the covered terrace

◐ *Fresh oysters are a local speciality*

of the restaurant. The owner is very friendly, and a simple meal can easily turn into an evening party with dancing. It's the oldest eating spot in the region, with oysters, mussels and lobster as its speciality. ⓐ Mali Ston ⓣ (020) 754 999 ⓦ www.vilakoruna.cjb.net

NIGHTLIFE

There's not usually much evening entertainment during the week – aside from the local colour at the hotels and restaurants – but Veliki Ston has concerts and other festivities on weekends. Check with the tourist bureau to find out what's on the agenda.

ACCOMMODATION

Hotel Bellevue ££ The hotel sits in a pine wood just 20 metres (22 yards) from a pebble beach and has a pool, restaurant and pizzeria. ⓐ Sv. Križ 103, Orebić ⓣ (020) 713 193 ⓦ www.orebic-htp.hr

Hotel Orsan ££ A 3-star hotel surrounded by pine and cypress trees on a quiet, sandy bay just a short distance from the sea. ⓐ Bana Jelačića 119 ⓣ (020) 713 193 ⓦ www.orebic-htp.hr

Ostrea ££ Classed as a family-owned 3-star hotel, but the nine rooms offered are more upmarket than others on the Peninsula – even including a 'presidential suite'. The hotel also has two good restaurants with a mouth-watering selection of seafood from starters to main (check out the menu on the web). ⓐ Mali Ston ⓣ (020) 754 555 ⓦ www.ostrea.hr

ⓞ *Croatia boasts more than 2,000 km (1,250 miles) of spectacular coastline*

Split

Split is a place that oozes atmosphere: little wonder, given that this major city actually grew out of a Roman emperor's palatial retirement home. Begun in AD 295, it took Emperor Diocletian ten years to build. The 'court' included living quarters for courtiers, a garrison to guard them, and soldiers to man the garrison. In total the fortified site measured 4,500 sq m (5,382 sq yards); the luxurious apartments of the palace were surrounded by lush gardens. After Diocletian died and left his mini-empire, a succession of despots gradually ran the palace into the ground over the next couple of centuries, until refugees fleeing barbarian invasions moved in and began to restore it.

Modern Split is the second-biggest city in Croatia, with some 220,000 inhabitants and tourism as its major industry. Many of these tourists come for the carnival season, when masked revellers take over the streets for the Feast of St Domnius in May. St Domnius is the city's protector (and patron saint of talented woodworkers), so the markets are full of craftsmen selling their wares during feast days. Split is a lively and friendly city; although it was not bombarded during the 1991 war, it did suffer from the huge influx of refugees and there was a big drop in tourism. Nowadays the visitors have returned. Tourist information has an office adjacent to the cathedral on the Peristil and here you can find maps of the city, ferry schedules and current phone numbers and addresses for local attractions, eating places, accommodation and so on. The office also sells the **Split Card** (ⓣ (021) 345 606 ⓦ www.visitsplit.com) that permits free entry or a discount for museums and galleries plus discounts on car hire, hotels and restaurants.

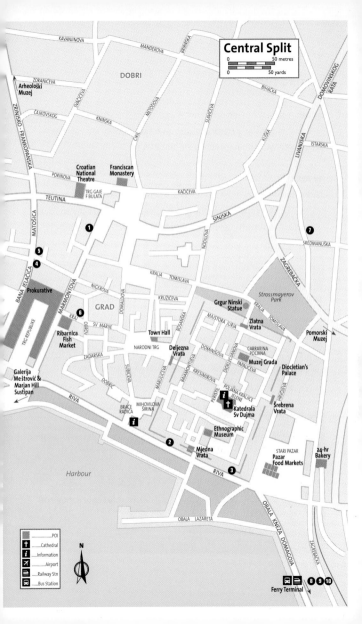

GETTING THERE

By air

Airlines fly regularly between Dubrovnik and Split
(see Ⓦ www.croatiaairlines.hr for details).

By road

There are frequent buses from Dubrovnik; the journey takes about
4 1/2 hours and should be booked in advance. The bus station is just
southeast of the city centre (ⓐ Obala Kneza Domagoja, Split).

By water

In the summer there are ferry connections between Korčula, Hvar (Stari Grad) and Split.

SIGHTS & ATTRACTIONS

Beaches

Locals usually journey out to the islands when they want to swim and enjoy the sunshine, but the main city beach at Bačvice is clean

The skyline of Split boasts a dynamic mix of ancient and new

and you can rent a sunbed and an umbrella there. There are also toilets, showers and bars near the beach. At Bene, on the Marjan Peninsula, there are some rocky coves and shady spots, plus showers and a refreshment bar.

Diocletian's Palace

For visitors, the main attraction is the Old Town, encircled by town walls with Diocletian's Roman palace at its heart. It's hard to get an image of what the palace must have looked like in the 4th century, since so much of it has been built around and incorporated into the Old Town centre. Little remains of the imperial apartments, although the medieval structures that took their place were built of the stone

○ *Diocletian's magnificent palace lies at the heart of Split*

DIOCLETIAN: EGOMANIAC EMPEROR

The Emperor Diocletian enjoyed pursuing grandiose plans and had a limitless passion for building; his constructions included basilicas, circuses, a mint, an arms factory and lots of grand houses for his relatives. Another of his major projects was the Terme di Diocleziano, the Diocletian Baths, a bathing establishment that was meant to outshine Rome's largest and most luxurious bath. Over a period of five years starting in AD 300, more than 10,000 Christian prisoners were used as forced labour to construct the massive edifice that was to accommodate 3,000 bathers with hot, cold and steam baths plus dressing rooms, gyms, meeting rooms, libraries and gardens. Marble façades graced the exterior and inside mosaic floors were part of a huge structure.

The emperor was born as the son of slaves in Dalmatia, possibly growing up in Salona. He rose up through the ranks in the Roman military and became emperor in AD 284 at the age of 39. Among his positive achievements were that he brought some stability and direction to a Roman Empire already under pressure from barbarian incursions. In an attempt to ensure the continuation of the Empire, he created a system of parcelling out authority for the Empire, dividing it into four regions, each separately ruled by an emperor. The power-sharing system soon disintegrated once he 'retired', however, and in fact led to his family's downfall. On the less savoury side, Diocletian is also remembered for his ruthless persecution of Christians: many of the country's saints were martyred at his command.

used in the palace. What used to be Diocletian's mausoleum now stands as **Katedrala Sv Dujma** (Cathedral of St Domnius ❷ Kraj Sv Duje 5), and the baptistery was once a temple. During the period between World War I and World War II, this whole area was badly run down and filled with émigrés and red-light bars – today, it's once again the centre of things, with lots of shops and tourists.

For anyone interested in Roman structures, there are maps available of the original palace and lots of detailed information on the temple, the cathedral, the underground chambers, the peristyle and the many altars. You can enter the area via one of four gates: Zlatna Vrata (Golden Gate), Deljezna Vrata (Iron Gate), Šrebrena Vrata (Silver Gate) and Mjedna Vrata (Bronze Gate).

Marjan

This nature reserve is located on a compact peninsula and is planted with a green assortment of Aleppo pines, cypresses, rosemary and holm oak. From Vidilica, there's a path along the south side of Marjan that leads to the 13th-century Romanesque church of Sv Nikola and the 15th-century church of Sv Jere, built on the remains of an ancient temple.

Pazar and Ribarnica (food markets)

The colourful open-air fruit and vegetable market of Pazar stands just outside the palace walls and is open every day. Since the people of Split haven't totally succumbed to supermarkets, this is where they shop for fresh produce. Photographers love the market and its wildly colourful assortment of peppers, tomatoes, melons, grapes, pomegranates and other delicacies. The Ribarnica (covered fish market) is nearby. ❷ Just east of Peristil, the Šrebrena Vrata leads onto Pazar ◷ 07.00–13.00 Mon–Sat, 07.00–11.00 Sun

Sustipan

For quiet walks, the cypress gardens of Sustipan have wonderful
views to the sea and Split plus some park benches on which to rest,
to exchange news or to meditate. You can see the foundations of an

⏺ *The idyllic gardens of Sustipan*

early medieval church called Sv Stipe (St Stephen) here in the remains of a Benedictine monastery. In the centre of the gardens stands a 19th-century neoclassical pavilion.

CULTURE

Arheološki Muzej (Archaeological Museum)

Founded in 1820, this is a well-displayed collection of Roman, Illyrian, Greek and medieval artefacts that includes jewellery, amulets, ceramics, glassware and coins. (Don't miss the lewd oil lamp!) Outside, in an arcaded courtyard and garden, there are pieces of decorative sculpture, sarcophagi and early Christian stelae. ⓐ Zrinjsko-Frankopanska 25 ⓣ (021) 329 340 ⓛ 09.00–14.00 Tues–Sun, closed Mon

Galerija Meštrović (Meštrović Gallery)

This monumental villa, built in the early 1930s, was chosen by Ivan Meštrović, the famous Croatian sculptor, as a summer residence and studio. He lived here until he fled the country during World War II. There are almost 200 sculptures on display, both inside the villa and outside in the gardens, in wood, marble, stone and bronze, and dating from the beginning of the century to 1946. ⓐ Šetalište Ivana Meštrovića 46 ⓣ (021) 340 800 ⓛ 09.00–21.00 Tues–Sun, mid-May–Sept; 09.00–16.00 Tues–Sat, 10.00–15.00 Sun, Oct–mid-May, closed Mon

Pomorski Muzej (Maritime Museum)

Divided into two sections – naval war and naval trading – this museum is intriguing even for non-sailors. There are model ships done to scale, naval paintings and lots of sailing equipment. Of special interest are

🔺 *The Meštrović Gallery houses works by the famed sculptor*

the world's first self-propelled torpedoes. Designed by Ivan Blaz Lupis, a Croat, and developed in conjunction with the British engineer Robert Whitehead, the model was successfully trialled in 1866.

🅐 Glagoljaška 18 ☎ (021) 347 346 🕓 09.00–13.30, 18.00–21.00 Tues–Sun, closed Mon

RETAIL THERAPY

For those who like antiques shops, **Antikvarnica** (ⓐ Cosmija 1, near
Sarajevo Restaurant) and **Anatik Shop & Galerija** (ⓐ Trg Cararina
Poliana) are worth some browsing time. For handicrafts, the market
in the cellars of Diocletian's Palace has a good assortment.

For high-quality Croatian wines, honey, olive oils and truffles,
check out the **Vinoteka sv. Martin** (ⓐ Majstora Jurja 17). More Croatian
wines are found at **Vinoteka Bouquet** (ⓐ Riva 3, east of Trg Republike).
For plain, everyday food of great quality such as *rakija*, buns and
cakes and wine, it is best to go to the market east of Šrebrena Vrata
(Silver Gate). The best place to buy snacks and fresh food is the daily
market at the eastern edge of the Old Town, where you can pick up
the ingredients for a picnic – hams, cheeses, tomatoes, lettuce,
olives, etc. If you need a bigger range of goods, the **Gavrilović**
supermarket (ⓐ Obala Kneza Domagoja ⓛ 07.00–23.00) is perched
at the ferry terminal. The 24-hour bakery **Prerada** (ⓐ On Zagrebačka,
opposite the market) intoxicates with its freshly baked breads,
cakes and strudels.

TAKING A BREAK

Babić £ ❶ This is a good place for a take-away pizza slice, the omnipresent
and delicious *pršut*, sandwiches and pastries. ⓐ Marmontova 7

Bobis £ ❷ For those with a sweet tooth, Bobis has a large café on
the Riva strip and a smaller outlet on Marmontova.

Ivona £ ❸ Croatian ice cream can be found in many outlets but
some of the best is here. ⓐ Riva 25

Kantun Paulina £ ❹ This is the place to get *ćevapčići*, a kind of spicy meat rissole beloved by the Croatians for snack food. ❹ Opposite Pizzeria Galija (see below)

AFTER DARK

RESTAURANTS

For a tourist town there's a curious shortage of high-quality restaurants in the Old Town, but there are a few outside the city walls. A good area to check out is on the western edge of the Old Town in the lanes west of Trg Republike. Restaurants tend to stay open until 23.00 or midnight.

Pizzeria Galija £ ❺ Excellent pizza cooked in a charcoal oven plus lots of pasta and antipasti. ❹ Tončićeva 12, a block north of Trg Republike ❶ (021) 347 932

Zlatna Ribica £ ❻ A stand-up buffet with cheap seafood snacks that are chalked onto a blackboard. ❹ Kraj svete Marije 12, right by the fish market ❶ 21.00 weekdays, 02.00 weekends

Konoba kod Jože ££ ❼ This cosy and intimate restaurant with fish nets on the wall is considered one of the best seafood restaurants in Split. Its risottos and pastas are a good bet and inexpensive. ❹ Sredmanuška 4 (heading north through Strossmayerov Park, this street is on the right) ❶ (021) 347 397

Stellon ££ ❽ In a country whose restaurants do mainly fish and meat, Stellon is a good option for vegetarians with its hearty salads and pasta and veggie mains. Smart, slick, hyper-modern interior but reasonably priced. ❹ Bačvice

Boban £££ ❾ For a gourmet meal, this is the number one choice – as it was for such luminaries as Placido Domingo. Croatian dishes are given an Italian twist in a nod to fusion cuisine with lobster done up as a spicy tomato stew and a fish carpaccio done sushi-style. Great wine list. ⓐ Hektorovićeva 49, parallel to Bačvice beach road Put Firula ❶ (021) 543 300 🕒 10.00–00.00 Mon–Fri, 12.00–00.00 Sat & Sun

Šumica £££ ❿ The emphasis here is on presenting the freshest possible fish and shellfish, but there are other choices on the menu such as a sophisticated version of the omnipresent schnitzel. The 'smart set' hangs out in this classy restaurant with its big outdoor terrace. ⓐ Put Firula 6 ❶ (021) 389 897

BARS, CLUBS & DISCOS

For what's playing, check the town website (Ⓦ www.visit-split.com), tourist information, the newspaper *Slobodna Dalmacija* or municipal posters displayed on billboards throughout the Old Town. These will also announce numerous open-air pop concerts that are held during the summer months. The nightlife scene in Split is not wild; it is particularly quiet in the summer, when a lot of people leave town for the islands.

Capo This is a café-bar at ground level that features a regular programme of rock, blues and cover bands three or four times a week. A 15-minute walk from the Old Town. ⓐ Bačvice beach pavilion

🅞 *Downtown dining in Split*

Ghetto Club Tables pepper an outdoor courtyard in the summer – there are occasional exhibitions and performances for the alternative crowd. ⓐ Dosud 10

Kanavelić For the 16–25 year-old age group, this is considered the 'in' place to be. Lots of techno music that spills out onto a crowded outdoor terrace in the summer. ⓐ Buvinina 1, opposite Prenošiste Slavija

Kocka An alternative club with a mixed programme of films, DJ nights and live gigs. ⓐ A 15-minute walk northeast of the Old Town, just off Slobode ⓦ www.kocka.hr

Metropolis This mainstream disco has been around for a while and features a mix of commercial, techno and rock with occasional live concerts. ⓐ Matice Hrvatska 1

Tribu A big favourite with the young crowd located on the main city beach, north of the centre near the Poljud stadium. ⓐ Osmih Mediteranskih igara 3 ⓣ (021) 384 745

ACCOMMODATION

Jupiter £ More or less a cross between a hotel and a hostel, the Jupiter has double, triple and quad rooms with shared bathrooms in the hallway. Good location and friendly. ⓐ Gravovčeva širina 1 ⓣ (021) 344 801

Adriana ££ Small, very conveniently located hotel with modern double rooms right above the seafront café-pizzeria of the same name. Very

comfortable and in high demand. ⓐ Obala Hrv. narodnog preporoda 8
ⓣ (021) 340 000 ⓦ www.hotel-adriana.hr

Bellevue Hotel ££ Overlooking the sea and comfortable and
convenient if not stylish. ⓐ Bana Jelačića 2 ⓣ (021) 345 644

Consul ££ On a quiet street near the Old Town with modern,
comfortable rooms and a summer terrace. ⓐ Tršćanska 34
ⓣ (021) 340 130 ⓦ www.hotel-consul.net

Hotel Marjan ££ A building that's been around for a long
time, but the rooms are still comfortable and well-equipped.
Friendly staff. ⓐ Obala Kneza Branimira 8 ⓣ (021) 399 211
ⓦ www.hotel-marjan.com

Hotel President £££ Lots of facilities with both plush rooms
and apartments, this 4-star property is a five-minute walk
north of the Old Town. ⓐ Starčevića 1 ⓣ (021) 305 222
ⓦ www.hotelpresident.hr

Park £££ A hotel with an exclusive feel to it and smartly decorated
rooms. Good quality restaurant with an international menu.
ⓐ Hatzeov perivoj 3 ⓣ (021) 406 400

Hvar

This is one of the most beautiful and popular offshore islands in Croatia, so it attracts tour groups from all over Europe. The capital, Hvar Town, has a 16th-century Venetian air, there are excellent beaches and the weather (according to fans) is sunnier and warmer than elsewhere. Locals insist there are 2,700 hours of sunshine a year and snow is rare. The main crop on the island is lavender and it's on sale everywhere – come in the spring and the air is heady with the scent. Wine is also produced, along with figs and olives.

Hvar Town, with its well-preserved Venetian Renaissance architecture, easily challenges Korčula and Dubrovnik in beauty, although the summer crowds can be a bit much. It's better to visit in the spring or autumn. The town wraps itself around a bay (Luca Hvar) and the main square, Trg Sv Stjepana, which is allegedly the biggest main square in Dalmatia. Beyond the town, stone houses clamber up three hills to a peak crowned by a Venetian fortress. After Dubrovnik, this is probably the most fashionable of Adriatic resorts for Croats who love to sit in the cafés of the main square. ⓦ www.hvar.hr

GETTING THERE

By water

The best travel links are to Split, with regular ferry connections from Stari Grad. **Jadrolinija** (ⓘ (060) 321 321, (051) 666 111 ⓦ www.jadrolinija.hr) runs a daily catamaran service that also stops at Hvar Town on its way to and from the island of Lastovo to Split. From Dubrovnik it is easiest to hire a car and cross on the ferry that runs from the mainland at Drvenik to Sućuraj on the eastern tip of the island. There are also links to Korčula in the south and thence to Dubrovnik.

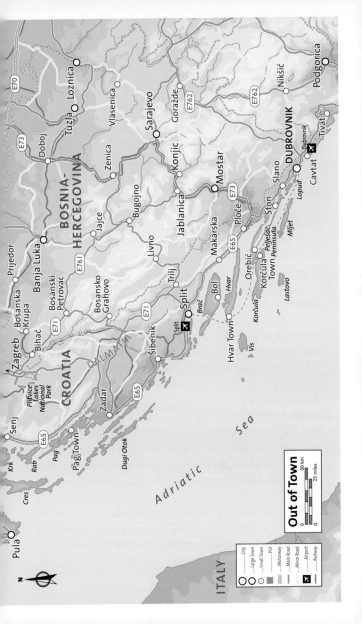

SIGHTS & ATTRACTIONS

Benedictine Convent

This is small as convents go, but the tiny group of nuns here spend their time making the extraordinary Hvar lace, which you see being sold in shops in Hvar Town. The nuns never leave the grounds and are bound by an oath of silence. ⓐ Northwest of Trg Sv Stjepana ⓣ (021) 741 052 ⓛ 10.00–13.00, 16.00–18.00 July & Aug, closed Sept–June

The Bishop's Treasury

Next door to the cathedral, this holds a small collection of reliquaries, embroidery and chalices. ⓐ Riznica ⓣ (021) 741 269 ⓛ 09.00–12.00, 17.00–19.00 July & Aug, closed Sept–June

Citadel

Built in the 1550s by the Venetians (aided by Spanish engineers), the building is called Španjola locally. Inside, there's a marine archaeology collection and a display of amphorae and Greco-Roman drinking vessels. The biggest attraction is the view from the ramparts.

Hektorović Palace

On the north side of the main square, this is a slightly spooky house that was left unfinished when it was built in the 15th century. Named after a famous poet, it has Venetian Gothic windows, and is one of the best examples of Venetian architecture on the island. ⓐ Northwest of Trg Sv Stjepana

Katedrala Sv Stjepana (St Stephen's Cathedral)

As a backdrop to the main square, this basilica was built between the 16th and 17th centuries on the foundations of an earlier

⬤ *The Pakleni Islands lie off the coast of Hvar*

THE ARSENAL – DRAMA FROM A CRISIS

This hulking 17th-century arcaded building dominates the square. It was where war galleys were once hauled out to be repaired. In 1612, the upper floor was converted into a theatre; it is the oldest in Croatia and one of the first in Europe. Check out the inscription inside – 'Anno Secundo Pacis MDCXII': this refers to the peace after a century-long quarrel between commoners and aristocrats. It followed an uprising in 1510 when 19 men were hanged from galley masts. The theatre was built to calm the distrust between nobles and commoners, since both classes shared theatrical space. ❸ Trg Sv Stjepana

monastery. It has a Renaissance trefoil façade and a lovely campanile; inside you can admire the 13th-century Madonna and child.
❷ Trg Sv Stjepana

Trg Sv Stjepana (St Stephen's Square)

Dating back to the 13th century, this imposing square opens onto the Mandrac, an enclosed harbour for small boats that leads to a larger bay. The old buildings lining the square have been converted into restaurants, galleries and small cafés.

AFTER DARK

RESTAURANTS

There's a full range of eating places in Hvar. Grilled fish and meat and black risotto are on offer, as ever, but local specialities include Dalmatian stewed beef, fritters, fig torte and octopus salad.

Bounty £–££ Reasonably priced grilled fish and meat with the mandatory seafood risottos. Try the excellent fish soup here washed down with the white house wine. ⓐ Fabrika, on the inner harbour

Macondo ££–£££ A first-class fish restaurant with faultless food and service – but be prepared to wait for a table. It boasts a small terrace for summer dining and a large open fire for colder nights. ⓐ Groda, in a narrow alley between the main square and the fortress ⓣ (021) 742 850

BARS

Carpe Diem Trendy cocktail bar that attracts all the 'beautiful people', so you'll be among friends. It overlooks the sea and has oriental wicker furniture and a plant-filled terrace. ⓐ Obala Oslobo enja ⓣ (021) 742 369 ⓦ www.carpe-diem-hvar.com

Cofein On the main square, there are tables outside almost all year long. ⓐ Trg Sv Stjepana

Jazz Walk south from the main square through the jumble of streets to find this laid-back bar with its fish-themed décor.

Loco On the main square, this is the best of the youth-oriented bars in town. Stylish, relaxing and chic. ⓐ Trg Sv Stjepana

ACCOMMODATION

Local hoteliers have joined forces in order to try to lure visitors in the winter months: free board and lodging if the temperatures go below freezing during the day, and 50 per cent off if it rains for more than

three hours during the day. Whether travelling in the summer or the winter, it's a good idea to book rooms on Hvar well in advance. (See Ⓦ www.suncanihvr.hr for additional hotel information.)

Dalmacija £ A basic but comfortable 2-star hotel on the seafront, a five-minute walk from the centre. ⓐ Obala Ivana Lučića-Lavčevića ⓣ (021) 741 120

Podstine ££ This is a quiet, family-run hotel near a pebble beach about 20 minutes west of the main square. Seventeen rooms, each with a sea view and a lovely terrace restaurant. ⓐ Pod Stine ⓣ (021) 741 118

Slavia Hotel ££ A 3-star, three-storey hotel with en-suite rooms near the ferry dock. Breakfast is served on a terrace right by the harbour. ⓐ Obala oslobodenja ⓘ (021) 741 820

Palace Hotel £££ This 76-room 'palace', built during the Hapsburg era, sits on the edge of the main square overlooking the harbour. Amenities include an indoor heated swimming pool, massage room and sauna. ⓐ Trg Sv Stjepana ⓘ (021) 741 966

● *Lavender is the main crop on Hvar*

Pag

In any island beauty contest, Pag wouldn't even be a contender, but it does have qualities that make it well worth visiting. The island lies in the south of the Kvarner Gulf and is a stark and desolate place that looks like it couldn't possibly support any form of life. A small population (and three times as many sheep) do live there, however, and they produce two things that have made the islanders famous throughout Croatia – cheese and lace. Pag cheese is a hard, piquant sheep's cheese known as *paški sir* that tastes like a cross between old cheddar and parmesan. Its distinctive taste comes from a mixture of olive oil and ash that is rubbed into the cheese before it's left to mature and from the wild herbs (like sage) and the salty vegetation that the sheep eat. The cheese tends to be a bit expensive but it's well worth the price. Pag lamb is also delicious, with the same wild herb taste.

GETTING THERE

By road
The Rijeka to Zadar bus passes through Novalja and Pag Town twice daily in each direction.

By water
There is a bridge linking the south of the island to the mainland, and a ferry from Karlobag on the mainland to Pag Town.

SIGHTS & ATTRACTIONS

Beaches
The three main beaches are Straško, Zrče and Časka.

Novalja

This developed resort lies close to several good beaches, so it attracts resort-seeking tourists and the all-night party crowd. Zrče beach, 2 km (just over a mile) south of Novalja has become one of Croatia's hottest spots at night in the summer with clubs that stay open until dawn. The major historical attraction nearby is the Roman town of Cissa or Časka (largely underwater) but there is an underground aqueduct with sections that you can visit. You enter through the town museum, whose collection includes amphorae from a 1st-century Roman ship.

Pag Town

This is the administrative centre for the island and there's a mix of new and old. The town was actually established in the 15th century and has a medieval quality. The parish church of **Sv Marije** (❸ Trg Kralja

PAG LACE

Lace is Pag's most famous industry, and a craft that remains very traditional and non-commercial. Once prized by emperors as 'white gold', 'Pag lace' is a relatively new name. The work is painstaking and created using an ordinary darning needle; each piece is unique and done without a draft or plan. When it is finished it is firm, as if starched, and will stay that way even after washing. While you can buy Pag lace in shops in Dubrovnik, it's a special experience to purchase it directly from the women dressed in local costume who sit on stools outside their homes. Women dressed in black come into town as well in the mornings to sell their handicraft.

Petra Kresmira IV) is worth a visit, if only to see the rose window on the Gothic church façade that resembles the intricate pattern used in local lace. In Pag Town, there's a tiny **Lace Museum** (ⓐ Kralja Svonimira), just off the main square.

AFTER DARK

RESTAURANTS
Taverna Boškanić £–££ Looking down on Stara Novalja, this is where to meet locals over wine and great platters of *pršut*, *paški sir* and sardines. ⓐ Stara Novalja

Natale ££ Right near the harbour in Pag Town, this restaurant specialises in Pag lamb and seafood – and also great *palačinke* and pizzas. ⓐ S Radića 2 ⓣ (023) 611 194

Restaurant Steffani ££ This is in the heart of Novalja and very popular with the locals as well as visitors. The usual seafood and lamb along with some local specialities like snails. ⓐ Petra Krešimira IV 28

Hotel Restoran Biser ££–£££ This hotel restaurant has a terrace overlooking the sea and serves local fare, seafood and other Croatian specialities. ⓐ A G Matoša 8 ⓣ (023) 611 333 ⓦ www.hotel-biser.com

NIGHTLIFE
Novalja (see page 135) is where the action is and where young people head if they're looking for dancing, drinking, eating and socialising outdoors until the wee hours of the morning. There are a variety of clubs right on the beaches, so the party spills out onto the sand as DJs spin the latest in dance tracks. Each of the beaches

has its following, but everyone's favourite, and the Novalja hotspot, is Zrče beach.

ACCOMMODATION

Biser ££ On a good beach in Pag Town, en suite rooms (some with sea views), TV and air-conditioning. ⓐ A G Matoša 8 ⓣ (023) 611 333 ⓦ www.hotel-biser.com

Pagus Hotel ££ On a small beach and central, the Pagus has spacious en suite rooms. ⓐ Ante Starčevića 1 ⓣ (023) 611 310 ⓦ www.coning.hr/hotelpagus

Hotel Plaža £££ The 4-star Plaza in Pag has smart en suites plus other amenities such as a pool and fitness centre. ⓐ M Marulića 14 ⓣ (023) 600 855 ⓦ www.plaza-croatia.com

Valentino £££ Right in the heart of Pag Town, five luxury apartments with all the frills, including kitchenettes, hydro-massage showers and internet availability. ⓐ A Danielli 2 ⓣ (023) 600 800 ⓦ www.valentino-pag.com

Plitvice Lakes National Park

While this stunning park is closer to Zagreb than it is to Dubrovnik, it is well worth a stop either on the way from the airport in Zagreb or on the way back. It's the country's oldest and largest national park and is on the UNESCO World Heritage list of sites – and little wonder. Sixteen emerald-green lakes spill one into the other via cataracts and waterfalls of varying height; the limestone rock around and in the lakes is a veritable artist's box of colours. The largest waterfall, Veliki Slap, is almost 70 m (230 ft) high. The water in the lakes hits every shade of green and blue and tree-shaded paths border the main lakes. The lakes are set in deep forests still populated by bears, wolves and wild boar, and cover nearly 300 sq km (116 sq miles).

GETTING THERE

By road

Plitvice is about halfway between Zagreb and Zadar on the main road, with regular buses going from each of these and also from Split. There are two entry gates (Ulaz 1 in the north and Ulaz 2 in the south) each providing access to a different section of the lakes. Most of the park's infrastructure (hotels, tourist office, post office, restaurant) are closer to Ulaz 2. Getting back to Dubrovnik or Zagreb is a bit tricky since buses don't always stop, especially if they're full – you need to flag them down.

TAKING A BREAK

Lička Kuća ££ This is a rustic mountain chalet type of place with wooden tables and chairs that serves traditional Lika food like roast

lamb, spicy sausages and *đuveđ* (ratatouille flavoured with paprika).
ⓐ Opposite Ulaz 1 ❶ (053) 751 382

ACCOMMODATION

The phenomenon of the private room thrives as an accommodation
option here. These can be booked at the kiosks open in July and August

🔼 *The breathtaking scenery of the Plitvice Lakes National Park*

WATER AND WILDLIFE

Veliki Slap literally means 'the big waterfall', and big it is. This high wall of water is the park's main attraction and the dramatic focus of the lakes. Other highlights are the largest lake, Kozjak, and Labudovac Falls. The park is also rich in wildlife: alongside the bears and wolves live animals such as lynxes and otters, while birdwatchers can look out for rare species including the eagle, peregrine falcon, hoopoe, capercaillie and eagle owl. There are well-marked paths, walkways and bridges linking the main attractions; alternatively there are regular park buses and ferries for those who prefer a less strenuous day out.

and run by park authorities at both entry gates, Ulaz 1 and 2. At other times, the tourist office in the nearby village of Korenica will book private rooms (❶ (053) 776 798). The tourist office in nearby Rakovica (❶ (047) 784 450) also handles private room bookings.

Bellevue Hotel ££ Basic but not fancy hotel with 70 rooms (six singles) with en suite bathrooms. Popular with tour groups. ⓐ Plitvička Jezera near Ulaz 2 ❶ (053) 751 700

Hotel Jezero ££–£££ Built on high ground overlooking the lakes, this is definitely the most luxurious hotel in the park. Resembling a large mountain lodge, there are 210 rooms decorated in natural pinewood. There are tennis courts, a sauna, a bowling alley and a fitness centre. ⓐ Plitvička Jezera ❶ (385) 53 751 400

● *Many of Dubrovnik's visitors come by ship*

PRACTICAL
information

Directory

GETTING THERE
By air

The only year-round scheduled flights between the UK and Croatia are with Croatian Airways, which has daily flights from London Heathrow to Zagreb and once a week to Split. From May to October, Croatian Airways flies from Gatwick to Dubrovnik three times a week and Manchester to Dubrovnik twice a week. British Airways runs seasonal flights from London Gatwick to Split and Dubrovnik. The flights are not cheap although occasionally there are specials. The flights from London to Zagreb are just over two hours (and about 30 minutes longer to Dubrovnik).

Anyone willing to do a little digging and research can find a considerably cheaper way to get to Dubrovnik by using one of the many budget airlines such as easyJet or Ryanair; you can fly to a terminal in a nearby country and continue on by train or bus. easyJet, for example, has flights to Venice and Ljubljana, from where you can connect to Croatia by bus, ferry or rail. Another option (especially for travellers from North America, Australia and New Zealand) is to use a hub city in Europe and then connect onto Zagreb or Dubrovnik: for example, Lufthansa flies to Zagreb from various UK airports via Frankfurt, and Malev has flights from London to Dubrovnik via Budapest.

British Airways ☎ 870 850 9850 ⓦ www.britishairways.com
Croatian Airlines ☎ 0 208 563 0022 ⓦ www.croatiaairlines.hr
easyJet ☎ 0870 600 0000 ⓦ www.easyjet.com
Ryanair ☎ 0870 156 9569 ⓦ www.ryanair.com

Many people are aware that air travel emits CO_2, which contributes to climate change. You may be interested in the possibility of lessening the environmental impact of your flight through the charity Climate Care, which offsets your CO_2 by funding environmental projects around the world. Visit Ⓦ www.climatecare.org

By rail

Travelling to Dubrovnik by rail is another option if you want to include other cities and travel in a leisurely way, but it's not an inexpensive choice. Rather than buy a return rail ticket to Croatia, it's wiser to invest in a rail pass and plan your own itinerary via an international rail timetable (see Ⓦ www.thomascookpublishing.com). There are a huge array of rail passes available, many of which must be bought before leaving home, while others can only be bought in the country for which they are valid. Inter-Rail Passes (available only for European residents) are available for 16 to 22 days or one month, and can be bought to cover two zones or all zones (global pass): 28 countries are grouped into zones. Eurodomino Passes, also only available to European residents, are individual country passes that provide unlimited travel in 25 European and North African countries. The pass allows you anything from three to eight days' extensive travel within a one-month period on the entire rail network of the chosen country.

A useful website for any kind of rail information is **The Man in Seat 61** Ⓦ www.seat61.com. For **Rail Europe** call ☎ 0870 584 8848 or check out Ⓦ www.raileurope.co.uk

By road

If you're coming by car, the most common road route from the UK to Dubrovnik is to take motorways from the Channel coast via Brussels, Cologne, Frankfurt, Munich, Salzburg and on to Ljubljana. From here take ordinary roads south to Rijeka on the Adriatic and then the coastal road through Split and on to Dubrovnik. Another route would be

through France and Switzerland to Italy's Adriatic Coast and Bari, from where you can catch the ferry to Dubrovnik. The disadvantage of having a car is that parking in Dubrovnik is difficult and expensive: hotel car parks are full to overflowing and there is almost no street parking. The 'Sanitat Dubrovnik' mounts regular patrols to seek out illegally parked cars and will tow them away to a pound in Lapad.

If you're on a tight budget, the cheapest way to get to Croatia is by bus from the UK. Eurolines offers a return ticket daily from London to Zagreb that costs less than £200 and takes less than 34 hours to Zagreb and 38 to Split (two nights are spent on the road). The company also has a pass that links 46 European cities and will get you as far as Vienna – once there, you pay for an additional bus or train ticket to Zagreb or beyond.

Eurolines ☎ 0870 514 3219 in the UK 🌐 www.eurolines.co.uk

By water

There is ferry service to Croatia from several Italian Adriatic ports (Ancona, Bari, Civitanova and Pescara) run by four companies: Jadrolinija, SEM, SNAV and Adriatica Navigazione. If you're travelling by car, book well in advance especially in high season; if going on foot, you can usually buy tickets on arrival in Ancona or Bari. During peak travel times, there are also swift hydrofoil and catamaran services between Italian ports and Zadar and Split for passengers only. On overnight trips, you can pay less than £20 for a bed in a basic cabin. For timetables, contact the ferry companies:

Adriatica Navigazione ☎ (3941) 781 611 🌐 www.adriatica.it
Jadrolinija ☎ (385) 51 666 111 🌐 www.jadrolinija.hr
SEM ☎ (385) 21 338 292 🌐 www.sem-marina.hr
SNAV ☎ (3971) 207 6116 🌐 www.snav.it

ENTRY FORMALITIES

Holders of full, valid EU, Canadian, US, Australian and New Zealand passports can enter Croatia without a visa for stays of up to 90 days (South Africans require a visa, obtainable in Pretoria). For longer stays, visa extensions are available by crossing the border into Italy or Slovenia and then re-entering. Other nationals require a visa for a small fee. Non EU nationals must provide evidence of sufficient funds (at least £100 per day). Theoretically, all visitors are required to register with the police but this is now a formality handled by the hotel clerks.

There is no duty on non-commercial goods brought in by visitors up to 30,000kn, although it is wise to register very expensive camera equipment or laptops. Also allowed: up to 200 cigarettes, one litre of spirits, two litres of wine, 500 g of coffee, 250 ml of perfume and up to 15,000kn in currency. For details on the rather complicated arrangements for reimbursement of VAT and other details, see Ⓦ www.carina.hr

For further information on entry formalities check the Croatian Government website at Ⓦ www.mvp.hr

MONEY

The main unit of currency is the kuna, which is divided into 100 lipa. Coins come in denominations of 5, 10, 20 and 50 lipa and 1, 2 and 5 kuna. Notes (which depict Croatian heroes) come in denominations of 10, 20, 50, 100, 200, 500 and 1,000 kuna. The currency gets its name from 'kuna', the Croatian word meaning 'marten' – in medieval days taxes were paid in pelts from the animal – and 'lipa', meaning linden tree. The euro is the secondary currency now, replacing the German mark, and the government tries to keep rates of exchange steady. The kuna is not a fully convertible currency, so you will need to buy it when you arrive and exchange it when you leave the country.

● *The kuna is the main unit of currency in Croatia*

In main towns and cities, Automated Teller Machines (ATMs) are available to be used with internationally recognised cards. Check the symbol at the back of your card with those shown on the bankomat. Traveller's cheques can only be exchanged in a bank, and cash advances on American Express cards can be obtained from Atlas travel agency, wherever they have an office. Most commonly used credit cards (Visa, MasterCard, American Express, Diners and Sport Card International) are accepted in large shops, hotels, restaurants and resorts and can be used for cash advances in banks.

HEALTH, SAFETY & CRIME

Dubrovnik is a relatively safe destination with most food safe to eat and tap water safe to drink throughout the country. Croatians will tell you that they have the cleanest water in Europe and, looking at the crystal-clear lakes and rivers, you're inclined to believe them. No inoculations are required for travel to Croatia, but anyone planning to do some trekking in the mountains should investigate being inoculated against tick-borne encephalitis. (Spray generously with tick repellents and wear long trousers tucked into your boots and a hat.)

There is a reciprocal agreement between Croatia and the EU countries for free healthcare, but sometimes certain services are not available in the public hospitals and you will have to be treated privately. Since private care is not cheap, it's a wise idea to take out health insurance for major emergencies. Small medical problems are usually treated at one of Dubrovnik's pharmacies (*ljekarna*), where there is usually someone who speaks English. Pharmacies operate a rota system, so there's usually one open at night-time and on weekends (check the posting on the window of the pharmacy).

For more serious problems, head for the nearest hospital (*bolnica* or *klinički centar*). Normal hospital treatment is free to citizens of most EU countries on producing a valid passport. Hospitals are clean and well run, although there might be a shortage of Western drugs. The most common complaints seem to be sunburn, seasickness, insect bites and stepping on sea urchin spikes.

Croatia is relatively safe when it comes to crime, but petty theft can occur and the best defence here is common sense. Don't flash around a lot of money, don't carry a wallet in a hip pocket and don't wear expensive jewellery. It's a good idea to take out travel insurance before you leave and take photocopies of all your documents, credit cards, etc. Streets should be reasonably safe at night.

OPENING HOURS

The usual opening hours for shops is 07.00–20.00 Monday to Friday and 08.00–14.00 or 15.00 on Saturday. Food stores such as the supermarkets will generally stay open until 18.00 on Saturday and will open on Sunday mornings as well. Open-air markets are normally open from 07.00–13.00 Monday to Saturday and from 07.00–11.00

on Sunday. Clothing shops and bookshops are open from 09.00–13.00 and from 17.00–19.30 Monday to Friday; also from 09.00–13.00 on Saturday. These hours may vary in the summer months in tourist centres particularly. Banks are generally open from 08.00–17.00 from Monday to Friday and from 08.00–11.00 or 12.00 on Saturday. Usual hours at post offices are 07.00–19.00 Monday to Friday and 08.00–13.00 or 14.00 on Saturday. Pharmacies are usually open 08.00–19.00 Monday–Friday & 08.00–14.00 Saturday.

TOILETS

Every restaurant and bar will have a toilet, but it's a good idea to cough up for an espresso or drink if you do use their facilities. Public toilets (*zahod* or WC) in town are more difficult to find, but those that do exist are usually clean, well-stocked and hygienic. In trains and bus stations, the public facilities usually come with a small charge of a couple of kuna. Men use facilities marked *Muški* and women's are *Ženski*.

CHILDREN

Croats love children – their own and those of visitors as well. Children tend to stay up late and, instead of being left with a babysitter, will often accompany their parents to a late dinner in a restaurant. Croatian pizzas tend to be close to the originals from Naples and popular with kids. Ice-cream parlours are also popular with children.

The Adriatic waters are clear and fantastic for swimming, but be warned that many beaches are pebbly rather than sandy and there may be sea urchins about, so take jelly beach shoes for non-swimmers or younger children.

Boat trips are another effortless way of entertaining children. Most include lunch and a chance to swim. A trip in a glass-bottomed cruise boat is an ideal way of introducing children to the marine life of the area. Check out ⓦ www.korculainfo.com for the best options.

Festivals always provide family fun, particularly those aimed at younger audiences, such as the **Puppet Theatre Festival** in Osijek (ⓐ Children's Theatre Branko Mihaljević) held in early May. Children will also enjoy the Moreška sword dance (see page 9), performed through the summer in Korčula.

For visitors on longer stays there are wonderful kids' camps that offer highly creative arts programmes, sailing, language lessons and a lot more – see ⓦ www.adriatica.net/kids

COMMUNICATIONS

Internet

Using the internet is especially popular here, so there are plenty of internet cafés, tourist agency rooms with computers, or sometimes just a lonely computer in the corner of a bar (cost is usually around 5 to 20kn per hour). Top-end hotels have cable lines in the rooms. Some of the internet venues use a Croatian keyboard, so ask for help – web addresses omit the accents. In Dubrovnik, try:

Dubrovnik Internet Centar ⓐ Branitelja Dubrovnika 7 ⓣ (020) 311 01721 🕐 08.00–20.00

Holobit ⓐ Kralja Zvonimira 56 ⓣ (020) 352 121 🕐 09.00–00.00

Internet Bar 'NETCAFE' ⓐ Prijeko 21 ⓣ (020) 321 025 🕐 09.00–23.00

Internet Club & Call Shop Black Jack ⓐ Boškovičeva 3 ⓣ (020) 322 158 🕐 09.00–23.00

Internet Club & Call Shop Snoopy ⓐ Andrije Hebranga ⓣ (020) 14 411 🕐 09.00–21.00

Phone

Public phones use magnetic cards called *telefonska kartica* and these can be purchased at newspaper kiosks or post offices. Rates change according to the time you call, with peak times from 07.00–22.00; Sunday has a 50 per cent discount. For local directory enquiries call ● 988; international directory enquiries ● 902 and for weather ● 9166 or road help and conditions ● 987

Mobile phones from North America encounter problems in Europe, so an international mobile phone like the **Mobal World Phone** (Ⓦ www.mobal.com) is highly recommended. This is advertised as the cheapest way to use mobile phones abroad and it works in 140 countries once it's set up. There are no minimums, service charges or fees – you pay only for the calls you make. The calls you make are debited from your credit card. Each user has a lifetime phone number that can be reached in any of the 140 countries.

TELEPHONING CROATIA
To call Croatia from abroad you should dial your exit code (00 or other) followed by the Croatia country code 385, then 20 plus the local number for all Dubrovnik numbers.

TELEPHONING ABROAD
For the best rates, go to phone booths in post offices or kiosks rather than the hotel. Dial 00 and then the country code (UK 44; USA and Canada 1; Australia 61; New Zealand 64), then dial the number, omitting the first zero of the area code.

Post

Stamps (called *marka* or plural *marke*) can be bought at the *Pošta* (post office) – look for a sign of a yellow spiral with a triangle on the end. You can also buy stamps from newsagents and tobacco kiosks. Post boxes are canary yellow. Stamps for postcards sent to a destination in the EU cost 3.5kn (takes around five days); postcards to North America cost 5kn and take about two weeks. Letters are priced according to weight and parcels should be left open for inspection by the post office before you send them.

ELECTRICITY

Croatia uses 220 volts and round, two-pin plugs. If you need an adaptor, get one before you leave home.

🔽 *Bus routes are clearly marked*

TRAVELLERS WITH DISABILITIES

It was, ironically, the 1991 war that raised the profile of disabled travellers because of the large number of wounded and physically disabled people that the war created. In larger towns and cities, many public places, such as railway stations and airports, are wheelchair accessible, and there are a growing number of hotels that take wheelchairs into consideration. Tourism offices will generally check accommodation for facilities for a visitor, but it's wise to double check with the hotel itself.

Additional information in English is published in a guide by **Savez Organizacija Invalida Hrvatske** (ⓐ Savska Cesta 3 10000, Zagreb ⓘ (385) 01 482 9394 ⓦ www.soih.hr). **Holiday Care** (ⓘ 0845 1249971 ⓦ www.holidaycare.org.uk) has basic information on facilities for disabled people in various countries.

TOURIST INFORMATION

The main tourist information office in Dubrovnik will hand out maps and brochures as well as making bookings for concerts and other events. To reach this office, go through the Pile Gate and walk about 200 m (220 yards) up the hill to ⓐ Ante Starčićeva 7 ⓘ (020) 323 887 ⓦ www.tzdubrovnik.hr

To read up further on your destination before leaving for Dubrovnik, you can contact the **Croatian National Tourist Office** (ⓐ 2 The Lanchesters, 162–164 Fulham Palace Rd, London W6 9ER ⓘ (020) 8563 7979 ⓦ www.croatia.hr). Staff there will provide answers to questions plus supply lots of brochures, information about accommodation and maps of specific towns and resorts.

In Croatia, all towns and regions have tourist information centres and, while they can offer names and addresses for accommodation, many don't book on your behalf.

Most towns and resorts will have a website that you can look up, and most have an English version. Among the best are: Ⓦ www.adriatica.net, which has general information about Adriatic resorts with an on-line booking service handling apartments, villas and hotels; Ⓦ www.croatia.hr, which is the official website for the Croatian National Tourist Board and this offers a large amount of information from history to accommodation and dining to links to other sites; Ⓦ www.tzdubrovnik.hr, which is the best of the sites covering Dubrovnik and the surrounding area.

BACKGROUND READING

Balkan Ghosts by Robert Kaplan. As a political look at the tortured politics in the area, Kaplan bases his insightful comments on an extensive trip in 1990. A good read.

Black Lamb and Grey Falcon by Rebecca West. This is one of the classic travel books for the area and it has both fans and detractors. The first quarter of the book is about Croatia.

Café Europa by Slavenka Drakulic. One of Croatia's leading novelists, Drakulic's collection of essays has a section on Croatia and the flowering of nationalism.

Croatia: A Nation Forged in War by Marcus Tanner. An enthusiastic, balanced and totally thorough look at the general history of Croatia, written by a journalist who witnessed the country's break-up.

Explaining Yugoslavia by John B Allcock. For anyone curious about how such a disparate bunch of nations were pasted together to form Yugoslavia, this is a knowledgeable and stimulating historical account.

Emergencies

The following are emergency free-call numbers:

Ambulance ⓘ 94

Fire ⓘ 93

Police ⓘ 92

Public Emergency Centre ⓘ 112

MEDICAL SERVICES

Hospital

Roka Mišetića ⓐ Lapad, 4 km (2 1/2 miles) west of Old Town; 24-hour service ⓘ (020) 431 777 ⓦ www.bolnica-du.hr

Pharmacies

There are a dozen or more pharmacies (called *ljekarna*) in Dubrovnik, with three on Stradun alone. These two pharmacies take turns to be open 24 hours a day:

Kod Zvonika ⓐ Stradun ⓘ (020) 321 133

Ljekarna Gruž ⓐ Gruška obala ⓘ (020) 418 990

POLICE

The police are visible everywhere (in their blue uniforms), and occasionally they will stop foreigners to ask for identification: be sure you have your passport or identity card with you at all times. The police are extremely pleasant and helpful to tourists, but not all of them speak English.

Police Station ⓐ Dr Ante Starčevića 13 ⓘ (020) 443 739

EMERGENCY PHRASES

Help!
Pomoć!
Po-moch!

Please call an ambulance!
Pozovite hitnu, molim vas!
Po-zo-vit-e hi-tnoo, mo-lim vas!

EMBASSIES & CONSULATES

Although there is a British Consulate in Dubrovnik, most embassies and consulates are in Zagreb:

Australian Embassy @ Kaptol Centar, 3rd Floor Nova Ves 11, Zagreb ☎ (01) 489 1200

British Consulate @ Atlas Pile 1, Dubrovnik ☎ (020) 412 916

British Embassy @ Vlaska 121, Zagreb ☎ (01) 455 5310
@ british-embassy@zg.tel.hr

US Embassy @ 2 Thomas Jefferson Street, Zagreb ☎ (01) 455 5500

● *The magic of Dubrovnik at dusk*

WHAT'S IN YOUR GUIDEBOOK?

Independent authors Impartial up-to-date information from our travel experts who meticulously source local knowledge.

Experience Thomas Cook's 165 years in the travel industry and guidebook publishing enriches every word with expertise you can trust.

Travel know-how Contributions by thousands of staff around the globe, each one living and breathing travel.

Editors Travel-publishing professionals, pulling everything together to craft a perfect blend of words, pictures, maps and design.

You, the traveller We deliver a practical, no-nonsense approach to information, geared to how you really use it.

Editorial/project management: Lisa Plumridge with Laetitia Clapton
Copy editor: Paul Hines
Layout/DTP: Alison Rayner
Proofreader: Wendy Janes